THE
cookie
COLLECTION

ARTISAN BAKING FOR THE
COOKIE ENTHUSIAST

BRIAN HART HOFFMAN

THE cookie
COLLECTION

ARTISAN BAKING FOR THE
COOKIE ENTHUSIAST

83
PRESS

83 Press
1900 International Park Drive, Suite 50
Birmingham, Alabama 35243
83press.com

ISBN: 978-1-940772-63-9
Printed in China

contents

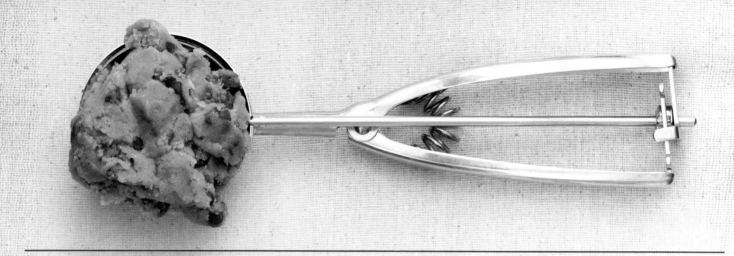

IT'S ABOUT TIME *BAKE FROM SCRATCH* CREATED
AN ODE TO COOKIES.

I'm beyond elated to say it, bakers: cookies are having a moment. Cookies have always been an essential part of my baking journey, my gateway recipe to the magical realm of dough. Now, with our premier cookbook solely dedicated to cookies, we're finally giving these humble heroes of the bake sale the sophisticated reevaluation they deserve.

The Cookie Collection features 128 of our all-time greatest cookie recipes, including 20 never-before-seen favorites. From the ease of drop cookies to the heightened elegance of Linzers, this cookbook has a cookie for everyone. For those in pursuit of the next big cookie—literally—look no further than our "Bake It Bigger" chapter, a love letter to the oversize cookie, including supersized renditions of some of my favorite cookies (looking at you Oatmeal Cream Sandwich Cookies, inspired by the famous Little Debbie version). For adults looking to blend the pleasure of cocktails and cookies, turn to the "Boozy Cookies" chapter for an assortment of baked goods spiked with bourbon, Irish cream, and rum. If you're looking for a deep dive into the supreme cookie, find our "Obligatory Chocolate Chip Chapter," which offers some tasty new tricks on an old standard.

Finally, there's the chapter closest to my heart, "FOMO Cookies." This term, dreamed up by my great friend, the all-around amazing baker Erin Clarkson (of the blog *Cloudy Kitchen*), highlights the cookies that evoke a baker's fear of missing out (FOMO). These are the have-to-bake-right-now recipes that keep us awake at night. This chapter has all the internet-breaking cookies you won't be able to resist, from gâteau Basque-inspired cookies to my own mash-up of apple-cinnamon cereal and snickerdoodles. Trust me, my obsession will soon be yours.

We go beyond offering foolproof, test kitchen-approved cookie recipes. Our goal is to help you master the art of cookie-baking, guiding you with our top tips and tricks to creating baked goods that look great and taste even better. We'll guide you from baking to storing and even let you in on how to properly package and mail your baked goods should a generous mood strike you. With this reference never far from reach, fabulous cookies are within your oven-mitted grasp.

What is it about cookies? Why do I turn to them again and again? In short, they're almost effortless, accessible, and always delicious. For that, cookies will never go out of style and neither will this cookbook. This is just the beginning. Craving even more cookies and epic baking content? Subscribe to *Bake from Scratch* magazine and find cookie inspiration in every single issue. Because cookies deserve more than just a moment—they deserve an era.

OUR BEST
COOKIE PRACTICES

1 INVEST IN THE RIGHT EQUIPMENT.

- **SPRING-LOADED SCOOP.** This handy tool allows you to scoop and drop consistently sized dough balls with ease and precision. Uniform cookies bake evenly; it's as simple as that.
- **FRENCH ROLLING PIN.** Tender doughs require a lighter touch than bread dough. Opt for a slim, wooden French pin. They're easier to maneuver than marble pins, and they apply delicate pressure to your cookie dough.
- **RULER.** This math class essential can help you measure the thickness of cookie dough when you're rolling it out so you always have evenly sized cookies.
- **COOLING RACKS.** Wire cooling racks allow air to circulate on all sides of the cookies once they're out of the oven to achieve a tender texture all around. When cookies are cooled on a plate, condensation gets trapped under the bottoms, making them soggy.

2 PROPERLY SOFTEN YOUR BUTTER. This is
essential to creaming butter and sugar because it helps incorporate air into the dough for soft, fluffy cookies. Check if your butter is properly softened by gently pushing into it with your finger. The butter should be cool to the touch, and your finger should leave a shallow indentation in the surface. If the butter is squishy and your finger sinks into it, it's too soft.

3 DON'T OVERMIX YOUR DOUGH. When
creaming your butter and sugar, spend about 3 minutes beating it until you reach the desired texture. Once you add flour, keep the mixing to a minimum. Every extra second spent beating your dough after adding flour activates more gluten, which means tougher cookies. Stir in your mix-ins by hand so that you don't overwork the dough.

4 CHILL YOUR DOUGH. This allows ingredients
more time to marry, creating a richer flavor, and prevents cookies from spreading too much while baking. After mixing, keep your cookie dough in the mixing bowl, and cover with plastic wrap. Chill in the refrigerator for at least 30 minutes. After you've shaped, scooped, or cut your cookies, place on a baking sheet lined with parchment paper, and freeze, uncovered, for 15 to 30 minutes. This final shock of cold before baking creates crisp, well-defined cookie shapes.

5 LIGHTLY SIFT FLOUR ONTO YOUR SURFACE BEFORE ROLLING OUT DOUGH.
Sifting the flour, instead of throwing it onto the surface by hand, ensures that you don't add too much. Excess flour on the surface will stick to your dough and lead to tough, dry cookies.

6 SPACE YOUR COOKIES OUT ON THE
BAKING SHEET. Leave at least 2 inches of space between each dough ball or more if recipe directs you to do so. This will give each one space to bake evenly and retain a uniform shape. You can be a little less generous with spacing the dough out for shortbread and gingerbread, which will spread less, but always leave at least ½ inch of space between each.

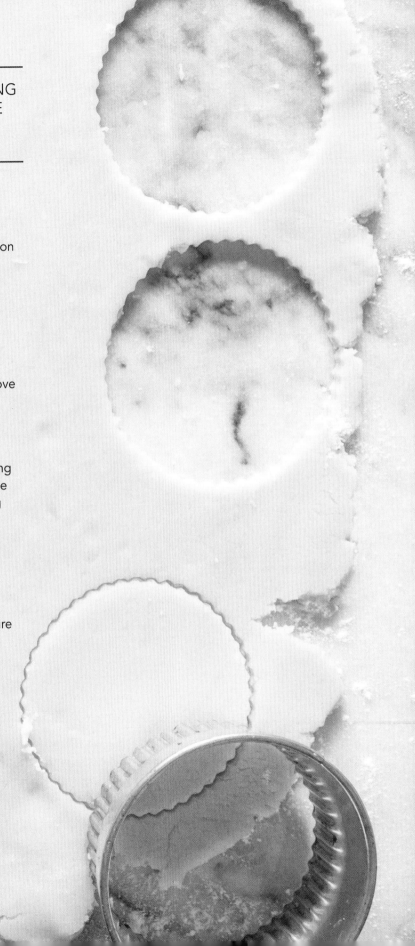

FROM PREPPING INGREDIENTS TO COOLING THE FINAL PRODUCT, OUR EXPERT COOKIE TIPS WILL HELP YOU BAKE THE PERFECT BATCH EVERY TIME

7 LET YOUR BAKING SHEET COOL COMPLETELY before placing a new batch of cookies on it. Placing cookies on a hot baking sheet can cause them to spread more as they bake because the heat melts the butter faster than the cookies bake.

8 DOUBLE UP ON BAKING SHEETS. If your cookies are browning too much on the bottom, stack a second baking sheet under the first one. You can also move your baking sheet to a higher rack in the oven.

9 LET COOKIES REST ON THE COOKIE SHEET for 2 to 3 minutes after baking before transferring to a cooling rack. Don't leave your finished cookies on the still-hot sheet for more than 5 minutes; you'll risk burning the bottoms.

10 NEVER STORE COOKIES WARM, OR THEY WILL BECOME SOGGY. Once cookies are completely cool, stack in an airtight container between pieces of parchment paper, and store at room temperature for up to 2 weeks. Store decorated cookies the same way for up to 1 week. Make sure to store soft cookies such as oatmeal cookies or macaroons separately from crisp ones, like lace cookies or langues de chat. This prevents the moisture of chewy cookies from softening the crisp ones.

FREEZER STASH

GET **COOKIES ON DEMAND** WITH OUR GUIDE TO
FREEZING DOUGH AND BAKED COOKIES

FREEZING COOKIE DOUGH: Most cookie doughs can be frozen, especially doughs that contain a high fat content, like drop cookies or shortbread. Delicate cookies with liquid batters, like lace cookies or madeleines, do not hold up well in the freezer.

- **DROP COOKIE DOUGH:** Shape your dough into balls, and place on a baking sheet lined with parchment paper. Freeze until frozen, about 6 hours. Place the dough balls in plastic freezer bags, and freeze for up to 3 months.

- **SLICE-AND-BAKE COOKIE DOUGH:** Tightly roll your log-shaped dough burrito style in plastic wrap, and twist the ends to seal it. Place it in a plastic freezer bag, and freeze for up to 3 months. When you're ready to bake, unwrap the dough, and let it thaw at room temperature for 10 to 15 minutes. This makes slicing easier and prevents the cookies from being too crumbly.

- **CUT-OUT COOKIE DOUGH:** Prepare the dough, and shape it into a disk. Wrap tightly in plastic wrap, and place in a plastic freezer bag. Freeze for up to 3 months. When you're ready to bake, let the disk thaw at room temperature until the dough can be rolled out.

FREEZING BAKED COOKIES: Shortbread, drop cookies, and sugar cookies freeze especially well. Once cookies are completely cool, place on a baking sheet, and freeze for 6 hours. Stack cookies between pieces of wax paper in airtight containers, and freeze for up to 3 weeks. To thaw, remove cookies from containers, and let them come to room temperature. Do not freeze baked thumbprint cookies or sandwich cookies with the filling. Add the filling once they're thawed. Do not freeze decorated or iced cookies. Instead, decorate after thawing.

SHIP YOUR COOKIES

DON'T LET DISTANCE KEEP YOU FROM SHARING HOMEMADE TREATS
WITH YOUR LOVED ONES. FOLLOW THESE STEPS TO MAIL YOUR COOKIES AND ENSURE THEY ARRIVE IN PERFECT FORM.

STEP 1: PROTECT THE COOKIES.
If your cookie is covered in sugar, icing, or another adornment, use plastic bags, muffin liners, plastic wrap, or foil to wrap cookies individually or in stacks of three or four. This will keep your toppings from falling off or smudging. There is no need to wrap sturdier, unadorned cookies, like biscotti. Simply stack or pack them in a tight line in the cookie tin.

STEP 2: PLACE THE COOKIES.
We like to mail cookies in tin containers because they're lightweight yet durable. Place a small layer of bubble wrap on the bottom of your tin for insulation. Cover the bubble wrap with a sheet of wax or parchment paper. Pack cookies tightly into the tin, filling any excess space with crumpled wax paper or bubble wrap. You want your cookies to have zero room to wiggle around in the tin. Place another layer of wax or parchment paper on top of the cookies, followed by a final sheet of bubble wrap. Cover your tin with the top, and tape it down.

STEP 3: PACKAGE THE COOKIES.
Select a box that is slightly larger than your cookie tin, ideally one that can give 2 inches of insulation on all sides around the tin. Use packing peanuts, bubble wrap, or brown packing paper to place a nice 2-inch layer in the bottom of your box. Place your cookie tin in the center of the box, and fill up any remaining space with more packing peanuts, bubble wrap, or packing paper. Your tin should fit snugly in the middle of the box with no space to move around. Tightly tape your box shut. Bonus points: Slap a "fragile" sticker onto your package so that handlers know your box contains precious cargo.

STEP 4: SHIP THE COOKIES.
Choose priority mail or two-day shipping to ensure your loved ones receive the freshest cookies. If you know the cookies will stay relatively fresh for a week, you can go with regular five-day shipping; just double-check with your carrier service to make sure they can get your cookies to the intended recipient in time.

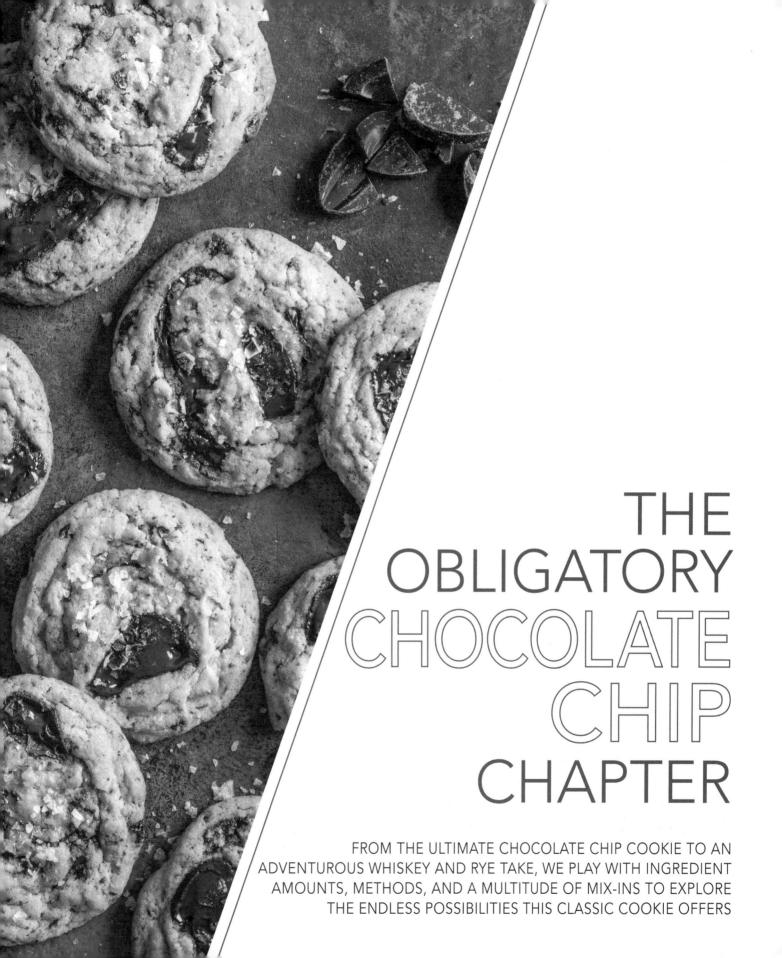

THE OBLIGATORY CHOCOLATE CHIP CHAPTER

FROM THE ULTIMATE CHOCOLATE CHIP COOKIE TO AN ADVENTUROUS WHISKEY AND RYE TAKE, WE PLAY WITH INGREDIENT AMOUNTS, METHODS, AND A MULTITUDE OF MIX-INS TO EXPLORE THE ENDLESS POSSIBILITIES THIS CLASSIC COOKIE OFFERS

[chocolate chip]

CHOCOLATE CHIP GRAHAM SANDWICH COOKIES

Makes 17 sandwich cookies

As a child, every time I spent the night with my grandparents Mimi and Grandad, Mimi served me a bowl of graham crackers broken into pieces with milk poured on top, cereal style. Made with graham flour and honey, this revamped artisan cookie was inspired by those flavor profiles and my love of a big ole chocolate chip cookie. The rich Vanilla Buttercream filling stands in for the milk in this epic sandwich cookie.

1   cup (227 grams) unsalted butter, softened
½   cup (100 grams) granulated sugar
¾   cup (165 grams) firmly packed dark brown sugar
1   tablespoon (21 grams) honey
2   large eggs (100 grams)
1   teaspoon (4 grams) vanilla extract
2¼   cups (281 grams) all-purpose flour
1   cup (135 grams) graham flour
1   teaspoon (5 grams) baking powder
1   teaspoon (3 grams) kosher salt
¾   teaspoon (3.75 grams) baking soda
2   cups (340 grams) chopped 60% cacao semisweet chocolate
Vanilla Buttercream (recipe follows)

1. Preheat oven to 375°F (190°C). Line 3 baking sheets with parchment paper.
2. In the bowl of a stand mixer fitted with the paddle attachment, beat butter and sugars at medium speed until fluffy, 2 to 3 minutes, stopping to scrape sides of bowl. Beat in honey. Add eggs, one at a time, beating well after each addition. Beat in vanilla.
3. In a medium bowl, whisk together flours, baking powder, salt, and baking soda. With mixer on low speed, gradually add flour mixture to butter mixture, beating just until combined. Stir in chopped chocolate. Using a 2-tablespoon scoop, scoop dough (about 40 grams each), and place at least 2 inches apart on prepared pans.
4. Bake until lightly golden, about 8 minutes, rotating pans halfway through baking. Let cool on pans for 5 minutes. Let cool completely on wire racks.
5. Place Vanilla Buttercream in a piping bag fitted with a closed star piping tip (Ateco #847). Pipe Vanilla Buttercream in a spiral starting at center on flat side of half of cookies. Place remaining cookies, flat side down, on top of buttercream. Refrigerate until set, about 30 minutes.

VANILLA BUTTERCREAM
Makes about 3 cups

1   cup (227 grams) unsalted butter, softened
1   tablespoon (18 grams) vanilla bean paste
⅛   teaspoon kosher salt
4   cups (480 grams) confectioners' sugar
1   tablespoon (15 grams) whole milk

1. In the bowl of a stand mixer fitted with the paddle attachment, beat butter at medium speed until creamy, about 2 minutes. Beat in vanilla bean paste and salt. Gradually add confectioners' sugar in two additions alternately with milk, beating until smooth. Use immediately.

CHOCOLATE CHIP COOKIE CUPS

Makes 18 cookies

If you're on the hunt for the best chewy cookie, look no further than this recipe. Studded with pecans and chunks of white chocolate and dark chocolate, these cookies are baked in a muffin tin to yield a pillowy center and crisp, caramelized edges.

1 cup (227 grams) unsalted butter, softened
¾ cup (165 grams) firmly packed dark brown sugar
¾ cup (150 grams) granulated sugar
2 large eggs (100 grams)
1 large egg yolk (19 grams)
2 teaspoons (8 grams) vanilla extract
2¾ cups (344 grams) all-purpose flour
1 teaspoon (5 grams) baking powder
1 teaspoon (3 grams) kosher salt
¼ teaspoon baking soda
¾ cup (128 grams) chopped 66% cacao dark chocolate*
¾ cup (128 grams) chopped 35% cacao white chocolate*
½ cup (57 grams) chopped pecans

1. In the bowl of a stand mixer fitted with the paddle attachment, beat butter and sugars at medium speed until fluffy, 2 to 3 minutes, stopping to scrape sides of bowl. Add eggs and egg yolk, one at a time, beating well after each addition. Beat in vanilla.
2. In a medium bowl, whisk together flour, baking powder, salt, and baking soda. With mixer on low speed, add flour mixture to butter mixture in two additions, beating just until combined. Beat in chopped chocolates and pecans. Scoop ¼ cup (71 grams) dough into each of 18 muffin cups. Cover and refrigerate for at least 2 hours or overnight.
3. Preheat oven to 350°F (180°C).
4. Bake until edges start turning golden, about 22 minutes. Cover with foil, and bake until centers are set, 10 to 13 minutes more. Let cool in pans for 10 minutes. Remove from pans, and let cool completely on wire racks. Serve warm or at room temperature.

*We used Valrhona Caraïbe 66% Cacao Chocolate Feves and Valrhona Ivoire 35% Cacao White Chocolate Feves.

PRO TIP
For lighter cookies, wrap outside of pans with foil, shiny side out, before baking. For more melty chocolate on top of cookies, press additional dark and white chocolate pieces in top of dough before baking.

[chocolate chip]

TAHINI AND MILK CHOCOLATE CHIP COOKIES

Makes about 48 cookies

Recipe by Ben Mims

Chocolate chip cookies don't need any improving, but this tahini version balances the sometimes too-sweet cookie and gives it a brittle, crunchier texture. The milk chocolate chunks are superior to dark chocolate, offering a creamy complement to the lean-tasting tahini.

1½	cups (330 grams) firmly packed dark brown sugar
1	cup (256 grams) tahini
1	cup (227 grams) unsalted butter, melted and cooled
1	teaspoon (4 grams) vanilla extract
2	large eggs (100 grams)
2½	cups (313 grams) all-purpose flour
1	teaspoon (3 grams) kosher salt
¾	teaspoon (3.75 grams) baking soda
9	ounces (250 grams) milk chocolate, roughly chopped

Garnish: sesame seeds

1. In a large bowl, stir together brown sugar, tahini, melted butter, and vanilla with a wooden spoon until smooth. Add eggs, and stir until combined.
2. In a medium bowl, whisk together flour, salt, and baking soda. Add flour mixture to sugar mixture, stirring just until combined. Stir in chopped chocolate. Refrigerate for at least 1 hour or overnight.
3. Preheat oven to 350°F (180°C).
4. Using a 1-ounce spring-loaded scoop or heaping tablespoon, scoop dough, and roll into smooth balls. Place 12 balls each on 2 ungreased baking sheets. Lightly press each ball with the palm of your hand, and sprinkle with a pinch of sesame seeds, if desired.
5. Bake until set and lightly browned at the edges, 10 to 15 minutes, rotating pans front to back and top to bottom halfway through baking. Let cool on pans for 1 minute. Remove from pans, and let cool completely on wire racks. Repeat with remaining dough. Store in an airtight container for up to 5 days.

Photo and styling by Mason + Dixon

PRO TIP
Allowing this cookie dough to rest overnight isn't essential, but it dramatically improves the texture of the cookies. If you like, simply refrigerate the dough for 1 hour, and proceed with the recipe.

S'MORES CHOCOLATE CHUNK COOKIES

Makes about 30 cookies

Recipe by Marian Cooper Cairns

We fused all the flavors of the classic campfire treat into one dough. In the mood for ice cream sandwiches? Vanilla bean, rocky road, and fudge will all be delicious sandwiched between these chewy yet crispy-in-the-right-places cookies.

¾   cup (170 grams) unsalted butter, softened
1   cup (220 grams) firmly packed dark brown sugar
⅓   cup (67 grams) granulated sugar
2   large eggs (100 grams)
2   teaspoons (8 grams) vanilla extract
2   cups (250 grams) all-purpose flour
1   cup (130 grams) graham cracker crumbs
1   teaspoon (5 grams) baking soda
1   teaspoon (3 grams) kosher salt
2⅓   cups (397 grams) chocolate chunks
1   cup (51 grams) miniature marshmallows bits*

1. Preheat oven to 350°F (180°C). Line 2 baking sheets with parchment paper.
2. In the bowl of a stand mixer fitted with the paddle attachment, beat butter and sugars at medium speed until fluffy, 2 to 3 minutes, stopping to scrape sides of bowl. Add eggs and vanilla, beating until combined.
3. In a medium bowl, whisk together flour, graham cracker crumbs, baking soda, and salt. With mixer on low speed, gradually add flour mixture to butter mixture, beating just until combined. Beat in chocolate chunks and marshmallow bits just until combined. Working in two batches, drop dough by 2 tablespoonfuls 2 inches apart onto prepared pans.
4. Bake until desired degree of doneness, 10 to 14 minutes. Let cool on pans for 5 minutes. Remove from pans, and let cool completely on wire racks.

We used Jet-Puffed Mallow Bits, a smaller, more dehydrated marshmallow product than regular miniature marshmallows. Do not use regular miniature marshmallows in this recipe. They will melt and burn.

Photo by Matt Armendariz

PRO TIP
To get photo-worthy cookies like the ones shown, press a few chocolate chunks and marshmallow bits onto the exterior of each dough ball right before popping them in the oven.

BROWNED BUTTER CHOCOLATE CHIP COOKIES

Makes 40 cookies

The addition of browned butter brings out the caramelized sweetness of chocolate chip cookies while imparting nutty notes to every bite.

1   cup (227 grams) unsalted butter
¾   cup (150 grams) granulated sugar
½   cup (110 grams) firmly packed light brown sugar
2   large eggs (100 grams)
1   large egg yolk (19 grams)
1   teaspoon (4 grams) vanilla extract
2¾   cups (344 grams) all-purpose flour
1   teaspoon (3 grams) kosher salt
¾   teaspoon (3.75 grams) baking soda
1   (11.5-ounce) bag (326 grams) milk chocolate baking chips

1. Line a rimmed baking sheet with parchment paper.
2. In a medium saucepan, melt butter over medium heat. Cook until butter turns a medium-brown color and has a nutty aroma, about 10 minutes. Remove from heat, and pour into a medium bowl. Place bowl in a large bowl full of ice water. Let cool, stirring every 5 minutes, until butter solidifies.
3. In the bowl of a stand mixer fitted with the paddle attachment, beat browned butter and sugars at medium speed until fluffy, 2 to 3 minutes, stopping to scrape sides of bowl. Add eggs and egg yolk, one at a time, beating well after each addition. Beat in vanilla.
4. In a medium bowl, whisk together flour, salt, and baking soda. With mixer on low speed, gradually add flour mixture to butter mixture, beating just until combined. Beat in chocolate chips. Using a 1½-tablespoon spring-loaded scoop, scoop dough (about 30 grams each), and place on prepared pan. Cover and refrigerate for at least 2 hours or overnight.
5. Preheat oven to 350°F (180°C). Line 3 baking sheets with parchment paper.
6. Roll chilled dough into smooth balls, and place at least 1½ inches apart on prepared pans.
7. Bake until golden, 8 to 10 minutes, rotating pans halfway through baking. Let cool on pans for 5 minutes. Remove from pans, and let cool completely on wire racks. Serve at room temperature.

THE ULTIMATE CHOCOLATE CHIP COOKIES

Makes 34 cookies

It's official: This is the perfect chocolate chip cookie. At once cakey, chewy, and loaded with melted dark chocolate, it's everything a chocolate chip cookie should be.

1   cup (227 grams) unsalted butter, softened
¾   cup (150 grams) granulated sugar
¾   cup (165 grams) firmly packed light brown sugar
2   large eggs (100 grams)
2   teaspoons (8 grams) vanilla extract
2¾   cups (344 grams) all-purpose flour
1   teaspoon (5 grams) baking powder
1   teaspoon (3 grams) kosher salt
¾   teaspoon (3.75 grams) baking soda
2   cups (340 grams) chopped 66% cacao dark chocolate*
Garnish: flaked sea salt

1. Line a rimmed baking sheet with parchment paper.
2. In the bowl of a stand mixer fitted with the paddle attachment, beat butter and sugars at medium speed until fluffy, 2 to 3 minutes, stopping to scrape sides of bowl. Add eggs, one at a time, beating well after each addition. Beat in vanilla.
3. In a medium bowl, whisk together flour, baking powder, kosher salt, and baking soda. With mixer on low speed, gradually add flour mixture to butter mixture, beating just until combined. Stir in chopped chocolate. Using a 1.5-ounce spring-loaded scoop, scoop dough (about 30 grams each), and place on prepared pan. Cover and refrigerate for at least 2 hours or overnight.
4. Preheat oven to 375°F (190°C). Line 3 baking sheets with parchment paper.
5. Place chilled dough at least 2 inches apart on prepared pans.
6. Bake until golden, about 8 minutes, rotating pans halfway through baking. Let cool on pans for 5 minutes. Remove from pans, and let cool completely on wire racks. Garnish with sea salt, if desired.

We used Valrhona Caraïbe 66% Cacao Chocolate Feves.

WHISKEY AND RYE COOKIES

Makes 26 cookies

With a splash of whiskey in the dough, consider this the grown-up version of a chocolate chip cookie. The rye flour brings earthy notes, and milk chocolate pieces round out the smoky whiskey with sweetness.

1	cup (227 grams) unsalted butter, softened
¾	cup (150 grams) granulated sugar
⅔	cup (147 grams) firmly packed light brown sugar
2	large eggs (100 grams)
1½	tablespoons (22.5 grams) whiskey
2	teaspoons (12 grams) vanilla bean paste
2¼	cups (281 grams) all-purpose flour
¾	cup (77 grams) rye flour
1	teaspoon (5 grams) baking powder
1	teaspoon (3 grams) kosher salt
½	teaspoon (2.5 grams) baking soda
1⅓	cups (227 grams) chopped milk chocolate

1. Line a rimmed baking sheet with parchment paper.

2. In the bowl of a stand mixer fitted with the paddle attachment, beat butter and sugars at medium speed until fluffy, 2 to 3 minutes, stopping to scrape sides of bowl. Add eggs, one at a time, beating well after each addition. Beat in whiskey and vanilla bean paste.

3. In a medium bowl, whisk together flours, baking powder, salt, and baking soda. With mixer on low speed, gradually add flour mixture to butter mixture, beating just until combined. Beat in chopped chocolate. Using a 3-tablespoon spring-loaded scoop, scoop dough (about 47 grams each), and place on prepared pan. Cover and refrigerate for at least 2 hours or overnight.

4. Preheat oven to 375°F (190°C). Line 4 baking sheets with parchment paper.

5. Place chilled dough at least 3 inches apart on prepared pans.

6. Bake until golden, about 10 minutes. Let cool on pans for 3 minutes. Remove from pans, and let cool completely on wire racks.

PRO TIP
For extra-chocolaty cookies, top chilled dough balls with more chopped chocolate before baking.

FOMO
COOKIES

"FOMO COOKIES," A.K.A. "FEAR OF MISSING OUT COOKIES," IS A BRILLIANT TERM COINED BY ERIN CLARKSON. THESE IRRESISTIBLE COOKIES CAUSE MUST-BAKE SENSATIONS. YOU'LL SUFFER FOMO IF YOU DON'T TRY THEM FOR YOURSELF.

CREAM-FILLED BASQUE COOKIES

Makes about 18 cookies

These indulgent cream-filled cookies embody the flavors of the gâteau Basque. A timeless cake from the Basque region in southwestern France, the gâteau Basque features a pâte brisée crust filled with pastry cream. We added crème fraîche to this sugar cookie base for a tanginess that complements the cookies' sweetness perfectly.

½   cup (113 grams) unsalted butter, softened
1   cup (200 grams) granulated sugar
2   large eggs (100 grams)
1   vanilla bean*, split lengthwise, seeds scraped and reserved
2½ cups (313 grams) all-purpose flour
½   teaspoon (2.5 grams) baking powder
½   teaspoon (2.5 grams) baking soda
½   teaspoon (1.5 grams) kosher salt
⅓   cup plus 2 tablespoons (110 grams) crème fraîche
Vanilla Pastry Cream (recipe follows)

1. In the bowl of a stand mixer fitted with the paddle attachment, beat butter and sugar at medium speed until fluffy, 3 to 4 minutes, stopping to scrape sides of bowl. Add eggs, one at a time, beating well after each addition. Beat in vanilla bean seeds.
2. In a medium bowl, whisk together flour, baking powder, baking soda, and salt. With mixer on low speed, gradually add flour mixture to butter mixture alternately with crème fraîche, beginning and ending with flour mixture, beating just until combined after each addition.
3. Divide dough in half. Roll each half between 2 sheets of parchment paper to ⅛-inch thickness. Transfer dough between parchment to refrigerator. Refrigerate overnight.
4. Preheat oven to 400°F (200°C). Line 3 rimmed baking sheets with parchment paper.
5. Remove top sheets of parchment. Using a 2-inch round cutter, cut half of dough, rerolling scraps as necessary. Using a 3-inch round cutter, cut remaining dough, rerolling scraps as necessary. With floured hands, place a 3-inch round in your palm. Place 1 tablespoon chilled Vanilla Pastry Cream in center. Top with a 2-inch round, and pinch edges of circles together to seal. If dough is too soft to handle, freeze until set, 10 to 15 minutes. (Using your finger, brush edges with water if there is too much flour.) Place cookies, seam side down, at least 2 inches apart on prepared pans.
6. Bake until bottom edges are golden and tops look dry, about 10 minutes. Let cool on pans for 2 minutes. Remove from pans, and let cool completely on wire racks.

VANILLA PASTRY CREAM
Makes about 1¾ cups

1½ cups (360 grams) whole milk
½   cup (100 grams) granulated sugar, divided
1   vanilla bean*, split lengthwise, seeds scraped and reserved
4   large egg yolks (74 grams)
3½ tablespoons (28 grams) cornstarch
¼   teaspoon kosher salt
2   tablespoons (28 grams) unsalted butter, softened

1. In a large saucepan, whisk together milk, ¼ cup (50 grams) sugar, and vanilla bean and reserved seeds. Heat over medium heat until steaming. Discard vanilla bean.
2. In a large bowl, whisk together egg yolks, cornstarch, salt, and remaining ¼ cup (50 grams) sugar. Gradually add warm milk mixture to egg mixture, whisking constantly. Return mixture to saucepan, and cook over medium heat, whisking constantly, until thickened and boiling, 4 to 5 minutes. Strain mixture through a fine-mesh sieve into a large bowl. Stir in butter in two additions. Cover with a piece of plastic wrap, pressing wrap directly onto surface of cream to prevent a skin from forming. Refrigerate until completely chilled, about 4 hours or overnight.

*We used Heilala Vanilla Beans.

SNICKERDOODLE SABLÉS

Makes about 24 cookies

Recipe by Marian Cooper Cairns

A sophisticated spin on the classic American cookie, this recipe delivers the buttery cinnamon flavor you love in a crumbly French shortbread. Instead of just rolling the dough in cinnamon and sugar like the standard snickerdoodle recipe requires, we incorporated the ingredients into the dough, brushed with egg yolk, and dipped them in cinnamon and sugar again before baking.

⅔ cup (133 grams) granulated sugar
2 teaspoons (4 grams) ground cinnamon
1 cup (227 grams) unsalted butter, softened
⅓ cup (40 grams) confectioners' sugar
½ teaspoon (1.5 grams) fine sea salt
2 large egg yolks (37 grams), divided
1 teaspoon (4 grams) vanilla extract
2 cups (250 grams) all-purpose flour

1. In a small bowl, combine granulated sugar and cinnamon.
2. In the bowl of stand mixer fitted with the paddle attachment, beat butter at medium speed just until creamy. Add ⅓ cup cinnamon sugar mixture, confectioners' sugar, and sea salt, and beat until smooth, about 1 minute, stopping to scrape sides of bowl. Add 1 egg yolk (18.5 grams) and vanilla, and beat for 1 minute. With mixer on low speed, gradually add flour, beating just until combined.
3. Turn out dough onto a lightly floured surface. Press and knead until dough comes together. Divide dough in half, and roll each half into a 7-inch log. Wrap logs in plastic wrap, and refrigerate for at least 4 hours or up to 2 days.
4. Preheat oven to 350°F (180°C). Line 2 baking sheets with parchment paper.
5. Using a sharp knife, cut dough into ½-inch-thick rounds. Brush top of rounds with remaining 1 egg yolk (18.5 grams), and dip in remaining cinnamon sugar mixture. Place rounds 2 inches apart on prepared pans.
6. Bake until golden, 18 to 22 minutes, rotating pans once. Let cool on pans for 5 minutes. Remove from pans, and let cool completely on wire racks.

Photo by Matt Armendariz

MILK CHOCOLATE EGG COOKIES

Makes about 30 cookies

A nostalgic ode to Easter candy, this Cadbury egg-studded cookie is all about the texture. Crispy on the outside, chewy on the inside, and with a boost of crunch from the candy-coated chocolate eggs, it's a new and improved way to indulge in the iconic Easter treat.

1	cup (200 grams) granulated sugar
½	cup (110 grams) firmly packed light brown sugar
4	ounces (115 grams) 45% cacao milk chocolate, melted
½	cup (113 grams) unsalted butter, melted
2	large eggs (100 grams), room temperature
1	teaspoon (4 grams) almond extract
½	teaspoon (2 grams) vanilla extract
1	cup (125 grams) all-purpose flour
½	cup (43 grams) unsweetened cocoa powder
¾	teaspoon (2.25 grams) kosher salt
½	teaspoon (2.5 grams) baking powder
½	teaspoon (2.5 grams) baking soda
2½	cups (450 grams) crushed candy-coated milk chocolate eggs, divided
½	cup (85 grams) 38% cacao milk chocolate chunks*

1. In the bowl of a stand mixer fitted with the paddle attachment, beat sugars, melted chocolate, melted butter, eggs, and extracts at medium speed until well combined.

2. In a medium bowl, sift together flour, cocoa, salt, baking powder, and baking soda. With mixer on low speed, gradually add flour mixture to sugar mixture, beating until combined. Add ½ cup (90 grams) crushed chocolate eggs and chocolate chunks, beating just until combined. Cover and refrigerate for at least 1 hour or overnight.

3. Preheat oven to 325°F (170°C). Line 3 baking sheets with parchment paper.

4. Using a 1-ounce spring-loaded scoop, scoop dough, and shape into ½-inch-thick disks. Place remaining 2 cups (360 grams) crushed chocolate eggs in a small bowl. Press each disk into candy eggs, coating well. Place 1½ inches apart on prepared pans.

5. Bake until set, 12 to 15 minutes. Let cool completely.

*We used Guittard Milk Chocolate Organic Wafers 38% Cacao.

BLACK COCOA SANDWICH COOKIES

Makes about 9 sandwich cookies

Just like the Oreo sandwich cookies of your childhood—only bigger, better, and baked completely from scratch.

¼   cup plus 3 tablespoons (36 grams) black cocoa powder, plus more for dusting
2   tablespoons (28 grams) unsalted butter, melted
5   tablespoons (70 grams) unsalted butter, softened
½   cup (110 grams) firmly packed light brown sugar
¼   teaspoon kosher salt
1   large egg (50 grams)
1   teaspoon (4 grams) vanilla extract
1½   cups (188 grams) all-purpose flour
Vanilla Filling (recipe follows)

1. In a small bowl, whisk together black cocoa and melted butter. Let cool slightly.
2. In the bowl of a stand mixer fitted with the paddle attachment, beat softened butter, brown sugar, and salt at medium speed until fluffy, 3 to 4 minutes, stopping to scrape sides of bowl. Beat in cocoa mixture. Add egg and vanilla, beating until well combined. Add flour, and beat until fully incorporated and a smooth dough forms.
3. Between 2 sheets of parchment paper, roll dough to ⅛-inch thickness. Transfer dough between parchment to freezer. Freeze until set, about 30 minutes.
4. Preheat oven to 325°F (170°C).
5. Remove top sheet of parchment. Dip a 3-inch fluted round cutter in black cocoa to prevent cutter from sticking to dough. Cut dough, leaving about ½ inch between each round. Discard scraps from around cookie rounds. Transfer parchment paper with cookie rounds to a baking sheet. (Reroll scraps between 2 sheets of parchment as necessary. Freeze rerolled dough for at least 15 minutes or until ready to cut cookies and bake.)

6. Bake until a slight indentation is left when pressed with a finger, 10 to 12 minutes. Let cool completely on pan.
7. Place Vanilla Filling in a pastry bag fitted with a round piping tip. Pipe Vanilla Filling onto flat side of half of cookies. Place remaining cookies, flat side down, on top of filling.

VANILLA FILLING
Makes about 2 cups

1   cup (227 grams) unsalted butter, softened
4   cups (480 grams) confectioners' sugar
1   teaspoon (6 grams) vanilla bean paste
⅛   teaspoon kosher salt

1. In the bowl of a stand mixer fitted with the paddle attachment, beat butter at medium speed until creamy, 5 to 6 minutes. Gradually add confectioners' sugar, beating until combined. Add vanilla bean paste and salt, beating until smooth. Use immediately.

SPICE IT UP
Black cocoa pairs well with spice, neither bowing to nor overpowering the warm, aromatic flavor. For a spicy update on the sandwich cookie, consider adding ¼ teaspoon to ½ teaspoon (1 gram) ground cardamom, cinnamon, or even cayenne to the cookie dough (after beating in the vanilla in step 2).

CHOCOLATE PEPPERMINT CRINKLE COOKIES

Makes 20 cookies

Recipe by Edd Kimber

If you like your cookies soft and fudgy, these are for you.

7   ounces (200 grams) 70% cacao dark chocolate, roughly chopped
½   cup plus 1 tablespoon (127 grams) unsalted butter, cubed
1   teaspoon (4 grams) peppermint extract*
1   cup (200 grams) castor sugar
¼   cup (55 grams) firmly packed light brown sugar
2   large eggs (100 grams)
1   cup (125 grams) all-purpose flour
3   tablespoons (15 grams) black cocoa powder
1   teaspoon (5 grams) baking powder
¼   teaspoon kosher salt
½   cup (60 grams) confectioners' sugar

1. In the top of a double boiler, combine chopped chocolate and butter. Cook over simmering water, stirring occasionally, until chocolate is melted and mixture is smooth. Remove from heat; add peppermint extract, stirring until combined. Let cool to room temperature, about 30 minutes.
2. In the bowl of a stand mixer fitted with the whisk attachment, beat castor sugar, brown sugar, and eggs at high speed until sugars are dissolved, about 1 minute. Add chocolate mixture, beating just until combined.
3. In a medium bowl, whisk together flour, black cocoa, baking powder, and salt. Fold flour mixture into chocolate mixture just until combined. Cover bowl with plastic wrap, and refrigerate for 1 hour.
4. Preheat oven to 350°F (180°C). Line 2 half sheet pans with parchment paper.

5. Using a 3-tablespoon scoop, scoop dough, and roll into balls. Roll balls in confectioners' sugar. (When rolling, you will want to compact the sugar onto the outside of the cookie because some of the sugar will absorb into the dough as cookies bake. If you don't add enough, you will lose the decorative look of the sugar. With only a thin layer of sugar, the beautiful cracking will be less pronounced.) Place on prepared pans.
6. Bake until lightly puffed and just slightly set around the edges, 11 to 12 minutes. Let cool completely on pans. Store in an airtight container for up to 4 days.

*I used Nielsen-Massey Pure Peppermint Extract.

Photo by Edd Kimber

PAN-BANGING MOLASSES ESPRESSO COOKIES WITH CHOCOLATE

Makes 10 cookies

Recipe by Sarah Kieffer

The pan-banging cookie has a devoted, wonderful fan base. Spiked with espresso and molasses, this cookie packs a bigger punch than the normal chocolate chip version.

¾   cup (170 grams) unsalted butter, softened
1½   cups (300 grams) granulated sugar
2   tablespoons (42 grams) mild molasses
1   large egg (50 grams)
1   teaspoon (4 grams) vanilla extract
2   cups (250 grams) all-purpose flour
1   tablespoon (6 grams) ground espresso
¾   teaspoon (2.25 grams) fine sea salt
½   teaspoon (2.5 grams) baking soda
4   ounces (113 grams) bittersweet or semisweet chocolate, chopped

1. Preheat oven to 350°F (180°C). Line 3 baking sheets with foil, dull side up.
2. In the bowl of a stand mixer fitted with the paddle attachment, beat butter at medium speed until creamy. Add sugar, and beat until fluffy, 2 to 3 minutes. With mixer on low speed, add molasses, egg, and vanilla, beating to combine.
3. In a medium bowl, whisk together flour, espresso, sea salt, and baking soda. Gradually add flour mixture to butter mixture, beating until combined. Using a spatula, make sure molasses is completely combined into dough and that dough is a uniform color. Add chopped chocolate, and stir to combine. Shape dough into 10 (3-ounce) balls, and place an equal distance apart on prepared pans. Freeze for 15 minutes.
4. Bake, one batch at a time, until cookies are slightly puffed in center, about 7 minutes. Lift side of baking sheet up about 4 inches, and gently let it drop down against oven rack so edges of cookies set and insides fall back down. (This will feel wrong, but trust me.) After cookies puff up again in about 1 minute, repeat lifting and dropping pan. Repeat 3 to 4 more times to create ridges around edges of cookies. Bake until cookies have spread out and edges are golden brown but centers are much lighter and not fully cooked, 14 to 15 minutes total. Let cool completely on pans. Refrigerate in an airtight container for up to 3 days.

Photo by Sarah Kieffer

EVERYTHING CHOCOLATE THUMBPRINT COOKIES

Makes 56 cookies

Dear chocolate lovers, you're welcome. To celebrate one of our favorite chocolate companies, Guittard, we used a few of our favorite Guittard products to create a sophisticated thumbprint cookie. These have cocoa powder in the dough, a pool of melty ganache in the center, and chocolate shavings and a light chocolate drizzle on top.

1	cup (227 grams) unsalted butter, softened
¾	cup (165 grams) firmly packed dark brown sugar
2	large egg yolks (37 grams)
1½	teaspoons (6 grams) vanilla extract
2	cups (250 grams) all-purpose flour
⅓	cup (40 grams) unsweetened cocoa powder*
½	teaspoon (1.5 grams) kosher salt
¼	teaspoon (1.25 grams) baking powder

Ganache (recipe follows)
Garnish: melted bittersweet chocolate, flaked sea salt, bittersweet chocolate shavings (see Note)

1. Preheat oven to 350°F (180°C). Line several baking sheets with parchment paper.
2. In the bowl of a stand mixer fitted with the paddle attachment, beat butter and brown sugar at medium speed until creamy, about 2 minutes, stopping to scrape sides of bowl. Beat in egg yolks and vanilla.
3. In a medium bowl, whisk together flour, cocoa, kosher salt, and baking powder. With mixer on low speed, gradually add flour mixture to butter mixture, beating until combined. Shape dough into 1-inch (13-gram) balls, and place 2 inches apart on prepared pans. Using a ¼ teaspoon, gently make an indentation in center of each ball.
4. Bake for 9 to 11 minutes. Remove from oven, and press down centers again. Let cool on pans for 10 minutes. Remove from pans, and let cool completely on wire racks. Spoon 1 teaspoon Ganache into center of each cookie. Drizzle with melted chocolate, and top with sea salt and chocolate shavings, if desired.

We used Guittard Cocoa Rouge Unsweetened Cocoa Powder.

Note: *Using a vegetable peeler, scrape blade lengthwise across room temperature chocolate to create shavings.*

GANACHE

Makes ¾ cup

⅔	cup (113 grams) chopped bittersweet chocolate*
½	cup (120 grams) heavy whipping cream

1. Place chopped chocolate in a large heatproof bowl.
2. In a small saucepan, bring cream just to a boil over medium heat. Pour hot cream over chocolate. Let stand for 1 minute; whisk until smooth. Refrigerate, stirring occasionally, until slightly thickened, about 30 minutes.

We used Guittard Eureka Works 150th Anniversary Limited Edition 62% Cacao Bar, but Guittard Semisweet Chocolate Baking Bar 64% Cacao will work, too.

TAHINI CHOCOLATE RUGELACH

Makes 24 rugelach

Recipe by Joshua Weissman

This traditional Jewish pastry is essentially a cream cheese-based sweet dough that's rolled with all sorts of fillings. Traditionally, rugelach is crescent-shaped, but I cut these into rounds instead. They are a little easier to make than the classic version, which means you get to enjoy them even sooner.

1   cup (227 grams) unsalted butter, softened
8   ounces (225 grams) cream cheese, softened
3   tablespoons (42 grams) firmly packed dark brown sugar
2   large egg yolks (37 grams)
1   teaspoon (4 grams) vanilla extract
2   cups (250 grams) all-purpose flour*
½   teaspoon (1.5 grams) kosher salt
1   cup (267 grams) tahini*, chilled
6   ounces (175 grams) 50% to 60% cacao chocolate, finely chopped
1   large egg (50 grams), lightly beaten
Sesame seeds, for sprinkling
Garnish: confectioners' sugar

1. In the bowl of a stand mixer fitted with the paddle attachment, beat butter, cream cheese, and brown sugar at medium speed until creamy, 2 to 3 minutes, stopping to scrape sides of bowl. Add egg yolks, one at a time, beating well after each addition. Beat in vanilla.
2. With mixer on low speed, gradually add flour and salt, beating until combined. Divide dough in half, and shape each half into a disk. Wrap in plastic wrap, and refrigerate for at least 6 hours or overnight.
3. Preheat oven to 350°F (180°C). Line baking sheets with parchment paper or nonstick baking mats.

4. Roll half of dough into an oval, ¼ inch thick. Using a bench scraper or a knife, cut edges to form a clean rectangle. Spread half of tahini onto dough, leaving a ½-inch border on all sides. Sprinkle with half of chocolate. Starting with one long side, roll dough into a tight log. Using a sharp knife, cut log into 1½-inch-thick slices. Place on prepared pans. Repeat with remaining dough, remaining tahini, and remaining chocolate. Brush slices with egg wash, and lightly sprinkle with sesame seeds.
5. Bake until golden brown, 20 to 30 minutes. Let cool on a wire rack. Dust with confectioners' sugar, if desired. Store in an airtight container.

*I used Bob's Red Mill All-Purpose Flour and Ziyad Tahini.

Photo by Joshua Weissman

RED VELVET PEPPERMINT SAMMIES

Makes 12 sandwich cookies

Recipe by Rebecca Firth

The chocolate flavor is really amped up in these by using both semisweet chocolate and Dutch process cocoa powder. This recipe will work with regular unsweetened cocoa powder as well, but the color won't be as rich and deep. When rolling the dough in the granulated sugar, take care to thickly coat it as this will help the confectioners' sugar adhere and make those high-contrast fissures that are so desirable in a crinkle cookie.

8	ounces (225 grams) semisweet chocolate, finely chopped
½	cup (113 grams) unsalted butter
1	tablespoon (15 grams) whole milk
1	cup (220 grams) firmly packed light brown sugar
1	cup (200 grams) granulated sugar, divided
2	large eggs (100 grams), room temperature
1	tablespoon (23 grams) red gel paste food coloring*
1½	teaspoons (6 grams) vanilla extract
1⅔	cups (226 grams) bread flour
½	cup (43 grams) unsweetened Dutch process cocoa powder
2	teaspoons (10 grams) baking powder
1½	teaspoons (4.5 grams) sea salt
1	teaspoon (5 grams) baking soda
¾	cup (90 grams) confectioners' sugar
	Peppermint Buttercream (recipe follows)

1. In the top of a double boiler, combine chocolate, butter, and milk. Cook over simmering water, stirring frequently, until chocolate and butter are melted. Remove from heat; whisk in brown sugar and ¼ cup (50 grams) granulated sugar. Add eggs, one at a time, whisking well after each addition. Add food coloring and vanilla, stirring until combined.

2. In a medium bowl, whisk together flour, cocoa, baking powder, sea salt, and baking soda. Add flour mixture to chocolate mixture, stirring to combine in as few strokes as possible. Let dough stand at room temperature for 15 minutes. If it is still too sticky to roll, refrigerate for 10 to 15 minutes.

3. Preheat oven to 350°F (180°C). Line several baking sheets with parchment paper.

4. Place confectioners' sugar and remaining ¾ cup (150 grams) granulated sugar in separate bowls. Scoop dough by 2 tablespoonfuls (28 grams), and coat heavily in granulated sugar. Roll balls in confectioners' sugar. Don't shake off excess. Make sure dough is covered well in both sugars. Place 2 inches apart on prepared pans.

5. Bake for 11 minutes. Let cool on pans for 15 minutes. Remove from pans, and let cool completely on wire racks. Spread Peppermint Buttercream onto flat side of half of cookies. Place remaining cookies, flat side down, on top of filling. Store in an airtight container for up to 3 days.

*I used Americolor Super Red 420.

PEPPERMINT BUTTERCREAM
Makes 2 cups

¼	cup (57 grams) unsalted butter, softened
2	ounces (55 grams) cream cheese, softened
2	cups (240 grams) confectioners' sugar, sifted
¼	cup (35 grams) peppermint candies, finely crushed
1	tablespoon (15 grams) whole milk
½	teaspoon (2 grams) peppermint extract

1. In the bowl of a stand mixer fitted with the paddle attachment, beat butter, cream cheese, and confectioners' sugar at low speed until smooth and creamy, about 2 minutes. Add crushed peppermint candies, milk, and peppermint extract, and beat for 1 minute. Use immediately.

Photo by Rebecca Firth

SPICED CHOCOLATE CHUNK OATMEAL COOKIES

Makes 24 to 30 cookies

Recipe by Thalia Ho

Filled with comforting spice, a drop of warmth from rum, notes of herbaceous rosemary, and molten bursts of dark chocolate, these cookies are stellar.

¾   cup plus 2 tablespoons (198 grams) unsalted butter, softened
¾   cup plus 2 tablespoons (174 grams) granulated sugar
¾   cup plus 1 tablespoon (179 grams) firmly packed light brown sugar
2   large eggs (100 grams), room temperature
1   tablespoon (15 grams) rum (optional)
1   teaspoon (4 grams) vanilla extract
1⅓   cups (167 grams) all-purpose flour
¾   teaspoon (3.75 grams) baking powder
¾   teaspoon (3.75 grams) baking soda
¾   teaspoon (1.5 grams) ground cinnamon
½   teaspoon (1 gram) ground ginger
¼   teaspoon kosher salt
¼   teaspoon ground cardamom
¼   teaspoon ground cloves
¼   teaspoon ground nutmeg
¼   teaspoon dried rosemary
2¼   cups (180 grams) old-fashioned oats
¾   cup (128 grams) very roughly chopped dark chocolate
½   cup (50 grams) rye flakes*
½   cup (57 grams) chopped toasted walnuts
Flaked salt, for finishing

1. In the bowl of a stand mixer fitted with the paddle attachment, beat butter and sugars at medium speed until fluffy, 2 to 3 minutes, stopping to scrape sides of bowl. Add eggs, one at a time, beating well after each addition. Beat in rum (if using) and vanilla.

2. In a medium bowl, whisk together flour, baking powder, baking soda, cinnamon, ginger, kosher salt, cardamom, cloves, nutmeg, and rosemary. With mixer on low speed, gradually add flour mixture to butter mixture, beating just until combined, about 1 minute. (Some dry floury pockets may remain in dough.) Using a large wooden spoon, gently fold in oats, chocolate, rye flakes, and walnuts. Cover and refrigerate for at least 1 hour.

3. Preheat oven to 350°F (180°C). Line baking sheets with parchment paper.

4. Scoop dough by heaping tablespoonfuls (about 45 grams), and roll into balls. Place 2 inches apart on prepared pans.

5. Bake for 12 to 15 minutes, rotating pans halfway through baking, raising pans a few inches above oven rack, and tapping pans firmly against rack to slightly deflate, spread, and help disperse melted chocolate into cookies. Repeat procedure every 2 minutes until cookies are just golden brown, firm around the edges and slightly soft in center, and have molten pockets of chocolate running throughout them.

6. Remove from oven; immediately sprinkle cookies with flaked salt. Let cool on pans for 5 minutes. Remove from pans, and let cool completely on wire racks. Best served warm on the day of baking but can be stored in an airtight container at room temperature for up to 5 days.

*Rye flakes are available at health food stores or online. You can also use ½ cup (40 grams) old-fashioned oats instead.

Photo by Thalia Ho

MACARONS

Makes about 36 macarons

Here's our easy-enough-for-beginners recipe for creating these pastel wonders at home.

1⅓ cups (160 grams) confectioners' sugar
1¼ cups (120 grams) almond flour
½ cup (120 grams) aged egg whites (see Note), divided
Gel food coloring*
½ cup plus 2 tablespoons plus ½ teaspoon (126 grams) granulated sugar
3 tablespoons (45 grams) water
½ teaspoon (2 grams) meringue powder
Desired filling (recipes follow)

1. Line the back side of baking sheets with nonstick baking mats.
2. In a medium bowl, sift together confectioners' sugar and almond flour. Add ¼ cup (60 grams) egg whites and desired food coloring. Set aside.
3. In a small saucepan, bring granulated sugar and 3 tablespoons (45 grams) water to a boil over medium-high heat. Reduce heat, and simmer until a candy thermometer registers 248°F (118°C), about 5 minutes.
4. Meanwhile, in the bowl of a stand mixer fitted with the whisk attachment, beat meringue powder and remaining ¼ cup (60 grams) egg whites at low speed until frothy. Increase mixer speed to high. Add hot sugar mixture in a slow, steady stream, being careful not to let sugar mixture hit sides of bowl. Beat until mixture is glossy with smooth peaks, 10 to 15 minutes. Gently fold almond flour mixture into whipped egg white mixture in thirds, being careful not to deflate egg whites.
5. Spoon batter into a piping bag fitted with a #10 or #12 round tip, and pipe 1½-inch circles 2 inches apart on prepared pans. Lift pan to a height of 6 inches above counter, and drop to release air bubbles. Repeat 3 or 4 times. Let stand at room temperature until macarons form a skin, 20 to 30 minutes. (Macarons should feel dry to the touch and not stick to the finger.)
6. Preheat oven to 280°F (138°C).
7. Bake for 18 to 20 minutes, rotating pans halfway through baking. Remove baking mats from baking sheets immediately after removing from oven. Let cool completely. (Shells may be placed in airtight containers and frozen for up to 1 month before filling and serving.)

8. Spoon or pipe about ½ teaspoon desired filling onto flat side of half of cookies. Place remaining cookies, flat side down, on top of filling. Refrigerate in airtight containers for up to 1 week, or freeze for up to 1 month.

We used Wilton Icing Colors in Leaf Green, Lemon Yellow, and Rose.

Note: *To age egg whites, place 8 to 12 egg whites (240 to 360 grams) in a medium bowl. Cover with plastic wrap, and let stand at room temperature for 3 to 6 hours. Alternatively, egg whites may be collected over the course of a week or a month and kept in an airtight container in refrigerator. Let egg whites come to room temperature before using.*

RASPBERRY CURD FILLING
Makes about 1½ cups

3 cups (390 grams) frozen raspberries
½ cup (100 grams) granulated sugar
1 lemon (99 grams), zested and juiced
3 large egg yolks (56 grams)
3 tablespoons (24 grams) cornstarch
¼ teaspoon kosher salt
4 tablespoons (56 grams) unsalted butter, softened

1. In a medium saucepan, bring raspberries, sugar, and lemon zest and juice to a boil over medium heat. Reduce heat to medium-low, and simmer for 5 minutes. Transfer mixture to the container of a blender, and blend until smooth. Strain mixture through a fine-mesh sieve; discard solids. Return mixture to saucepan, and heat over medium heat.
2. In a medium bowl, whisk together egg yolks, cornstarch, and salt. Add about ¼ cup hot raspberry mixture to egg mixture, whisking constantly. Add egg mixture to remaining hot raspberry mixture in pan. Cook over medium-high heat, whisking constantly, until thickened, 5 to 7 minutes. Remove from heat; add butter, 1 tablespoon (14 grams) at a time, whisking to combine after each addition. Refrigerate for at least 2 hours or up to 1 week.

CHOCOLATE-ORANGE GANACHE FILLING
Makes about 1 cup

1 cup (240 grams) heavy whipping cream
3 tablespoons (9 grams) orange zest
1⅓ cups (227 grams) chopped 66% cacao bittersweet chocolate

1. In a small saucepan, bring cream and zest to just below a boil over medium-high heat; remove from heat. Cover and let stand at room temperature for 30 minutes.

2. Strain mixture through a fine-mesh sieve; discard solids. Return cream mixture to saucepan, and bring to a simmer over medium-high heat.

3. Place chopped chocolate in a medium heat-proof bowl. Pour hot cream mixture over chocolate. Cover with plastic wrap, and let stand for 5 minutes; whisk until smooth. Refrigerate for 1 to 2 hours before using. (Chocolate should be pliable but not runny.)

BASIC BUTTERCREAM FILLING
Makes about 2 cups

½	cup (113 grams) unsalted butter, softened
3	cups (360 grams) confectioners' sugar
1	teaspoon (3 grams) kosher salt

1. In the bowl of a stand mixer fitted with the paddle attachment, beat butter at medium speed until creamy, 2 to 3 minutes. Gradually add confectioners' sugar and salt, beating until smooth. Use immediately.

Three Easy Buttercream Variations
Lemon: Add the zest and juice of 1 lemon.
Vanilla Bean: Add scraped seeds of half a vanilla bean.
Pistachio: Add ¼ cup (28 grams) finely ground pistachios, ½ teaspoon (1.5 grams) kosher salt, and 1 to 2 drops green food coloring.

APPLE-CINNAMON CEREAL SNICKERDOODLES

Makes about 18 cookies

Apple Jacks has always been my favorite cereal. I ate it for breakfast most mornings growing up, and as an adult, I've made it the official treat of my birthday—the only day of the year when I eat as many bowls as I want. With crushed cereal in the dough and a Cereal Milk Glaze, these chewy cookies are an ode to that, but I'll be making these far more often than just on my birthday.

½   cup (113 grams) unsalted butter, softened
1   cup (200 grams) plus 2 tablespoons (24 grams) granulated sugar, divided
1   large egg (50 grams)
1   teaspoon (6 grams) vanilla bean paste
1¼   cups (156 grams) all-purpose flour
½   cup (36 grams) plus 1 tablespoon (4.5 grams) ground apple-cinnamon cereal*, divided
1   teaspoon (2 grams) ground cinnamon, divided
¼   teaspoon (1.25 grams) baking soda
¼   teaspoon (1 gram) cream of tartar
Cereal Milk Glaze (recipe follows)

1. Preheat oven to 375°F (190°C). Line 2 baking sheets with parchment paper.
2. In the bowl of a stand mixer fitted with the paddle attachment, beat butter and 1 cup (200 grams) sugar at medium speed until fluffy, 2 to 3 minutes, stopping to scrape sides of bowl. Add egg, beating well. Beat in vanilla bean paste.
3. In a medium bowl, whisk together flour, ½ cup (36 grams) ground apple-cinnamon cereal, ½ teaspoon (1 gram) cinnamon, baking soda, and cream of tartar. With mixer on low speed, gradually add flour mixture to butter mixture, beating just until combined.

4. In a small bowl, stir together remaining 2 tablespoons (24 grams) sugar, remaining 1 tablespoon (4.5 grams) ground cereal, and remaining ½ teaspoon (1 gram) cinnamon. Using a 1½-tablespoon spring-loaded scoop, scoop dough into mounds (about 30 grams each). Roll each mound into a smooth ball, and toss balls in sugar mixture. Place at least 2 inches apart on prepared pans.
5. Bake until lightly golden, 8 to 10 minutes, rotating pans halfway through baking. Let cool on pans for 5 minutes. Remove from pans, and let cool completely on wire racks. Drizzle with Cereal Milk Glaze.

*We used Kellogg's Apple Jacks.

CEREAL MILK GLAZE
Makes ⅔ cup

½   cup (15 grams) apple-cinnamon cereal*
¼   cup (60 grams) whole milk
1½   cups (180 grams) confectioners' sugar

In a small bowl, soak apple-cinnamon cereal in milk for 15 minutes. Strain milk through a fine-mesh sieve into a medium bowl. Gradually add confectioners' sugar, whisking until smooth. Use immediately.

*We used Kellogg's Apple Jacks.

MALTED WHITE CHOCOLATE LACE COOKIES

Makes 36 cookies

Recipe by Kellie Kelly

Combining velvety white chocolate with the rich caramel notes of malted milk, these wafer-thin cookies have a buttery snap that you'll find irresistible.

1	cup (227 grams) unsalted butter, softened
1	cup (220 grams) firmly packed light brown sugar
2	tablespoons (42 grams) honey
1	tablespoon (13 grams) vanilla extract
1	teaspoon (3 grams) kosher salt
2	cups (250 grams) all-purpose flour
⅔	cup (80 grams) malted milk powder
1	teaspoon (5 grams) baking soda
6	ounces (175 grams) white chocolate, coarsely chopped

1. Preheat oven to 350°F (180°C). Line baking sheets with parchment paper.

2. In the bowl of a stand mixer fitted with the paddle attachment, beat butter, brown sugar, honey, vanilla, and salt at medium speed until creamy, 3 to 4 minutes, stopping to scrape sides of bowl. With mixer on low speed, add flour, milk powder, and baking soda, beating until combined. Add chopped chocolate; stir well. (Dough will be very stiff.)

3. Roll dough into 1-inch balls (about 30 grams each), and place 3 inches apart on prepared pans. Gently press each ball to ½-inch thickness.

4. Bake until puffed around the edges, about 10 minutes. Let cool on pans for 5 minutes. Remove from pans, and let cool completely on wire racks.

PRO TIP
Be sure to space the dough balls 3 inches apart, because the dough will spread during baking.

HUMMINGBIRD COOKIES

Makes about 43 cookies

Inspired by the timeless Southern layer cake and loaded with pecans, fresh bananas, and dried pineapple, these cookies are another way to celebrate the flavors of my favorite cake. A dollop of Cream Cheese Frosting serves as a tangy nod to the original. I love hummingbird anything, and these are hummingbird everything.

1   cup (227 grams) unsalted butter, softened
1½   cups (300 grams) granulated sugar
1   large egg (50 grams)
2   teaspoons (8 grams) vanilla extract
2¾   cups (344 grams) all-purpose flour
1   teaspoon (2 grams) ground cinnamon
¾   teaspoon (3.75 grams) baking soda
¾   teaspoon (2.25 grams) kosher salt
½   cup (114 grams) mashed banana (about 1 medium banana)
¾   cup (135 grams) diced dried pineapple
½   cup (57 grams) chopped pecans
½   cup (54 grams) banana chips, chopped
Cream Cheese Frosting (recipe follows)
Garnish: chopped pecans, dried pineapple

1. Preheat oven to 325°F (170°C). Line 4 baking sheets with parchment paper.
2. In the bowl of a stand mixer fitted with the paddle attachment, beat butter and sugar at medium speed until fluffy, 2 to 3 minutes, stopping to scrape sides of bowl. Add egg, beating well. Beat in vanilla.
3. In a medium bowl, whisk together flour, cinnamon, baking soda, and salt. With mixer on low speed, add flour mixture to butter mixture in two additions alternately with mashed banana, beating just until combined. Beat in pineapple, pecans, and banana chips. Using a 1½-tablespoon spring-loaded scoop, scoop dough (about 30 grams each), and place at least 2 inches apart on prepared pans.
4. Bake until lightly golden, 12 to 14 minutes, rotating pans halfway through baking. Let cool on pans for 5 minutes. Remove from pans, and let cool completely on wire racks. Top with Cream Cheese Frosting. Garnish with pecans or pineapple, if desired. Refrigerate in an airtight container for up to 3 days.

CREAM CHEESE FROSTING
Makes about 1½ cups

8   ounces (225 grams) cream cheese, softened
2   cups (240 grams) confectioners' sugar

1. In a medium bowl, beat cream cheese with a mixer at medium speed until smooth. Gradually add confectioners' sugar, beating until smooth. Use immediately.

SALTED CARAMEL SNICKERDOODLES

Makes about 46 cookies

Recipe by Erin Clarkson

A caramel-packed take on the classic holiday treat, this cookie has crushed caramel in the dough for extra chew while a final roll in cinnamon sugar gives it that classic snickerdoodle taste.

Salted Caramel (recipe follows)
1   cup (227 grams) unsalted butter, softened
¾   cup (150 grams) granulated sugar, divided
¼   cup (55 grams) firmly packed dark brown sugar
1   large egg (50 grams)
1   teaspoon (4 grams) vanilla extract
2¾   cups plus 2 teaspoons (350 grams) all-purpose flour
½   teaspoon (2.5 grams) baking soda
½   teaspoon (1.5 grams) kosher salt
½   teaspoon (1 gram) ground cinnamon
Flaked sea salt, for finishing

1. Break Salted Caramel into large chunks, and weigh out 1 cup (200 grams) caramel. Place in a resealable plastic bag, and break with a rolling pin until it forms small chunks. Set aside.
2. Place remaining Salted Caramel in the work bowl of a food processor; pulse until finely ground. Weigh out ¾ cup (150 grams) ground caramel. (The caramel, once ground, will pull moisture out of the environment very quickly and start to clump, so use the ground caramel fresh out of the food processor.)
3. Preheat oven to 350°F (180°C). Line several baking sheets with parchment paper.
4. In the bowl of a stand mixer fitted with the paddle attachment, beat ¾ cup (150 grams) ground caramel, butter, ½ cup (100 grams) granulated sugar, and brown sugar at high speed until creamy, 2 to 3 minutes, stopping to scrape sides of bowl. With mixer on medium speed, add egg and vanilla, beating until combined.
5. In a medium bowl, sift together flour, baking soda, and kosher salt. With mixer on low speed, gradually add flour mixture to butter mixture, beating just until combined. Stir in 1 cup (200 grams) caramel chunks until evenly distributed.
6. In a small bowl, stir together cinnamon and remaining ¼ cup (50 grams) granulated sugar. Using a 1-tablespoon scoop, scoop dough, and roll into balls. Roll balls in cinnamon sugar mixture. Place

2 inches apart on prepared pans. Freeze for 5 minutes.
7. Bake, one batch at a time, until golden brown and puffed up, 11 to 12 minutes. Let cool completely on pans. Sprinkle with sea salt. Store in an airtight container.

Note: *If you do not want to bake all of these cookies at once, the dough, once rolled in the cinnamon sugar, can be stored in a resealable plastic bag in the freezer. Freeze until solid on a baking sheet before transferring to a bag.*

SALTED CARAMEL
Makes about 2 cups

2   cups (400 grams) granulated sugar
1   teaspoon (3 grams) kosher salt

1. Line a half sheet pan with a nonstick baking mat.
2. In a medium saucepan, heat sugar over medium heat, whisking occasionally, until sugar is dissolved. (Sugar will clump as you heat, but continue to stir, and it will soon smooth out.) Cook until sugar turns amber colored and is just beginning to smoke slightly. Immediately pour onto prepared pan, and sprinkle with salt. Let cool completely.

Photo by Erin Clarkson

PRO TIP
Have everything ready to go for the Salted Caramel. There are a few seconds between a toasty caramel and a burnt sugar, so you want to be able to pour out the caramel as soon as it is ready.

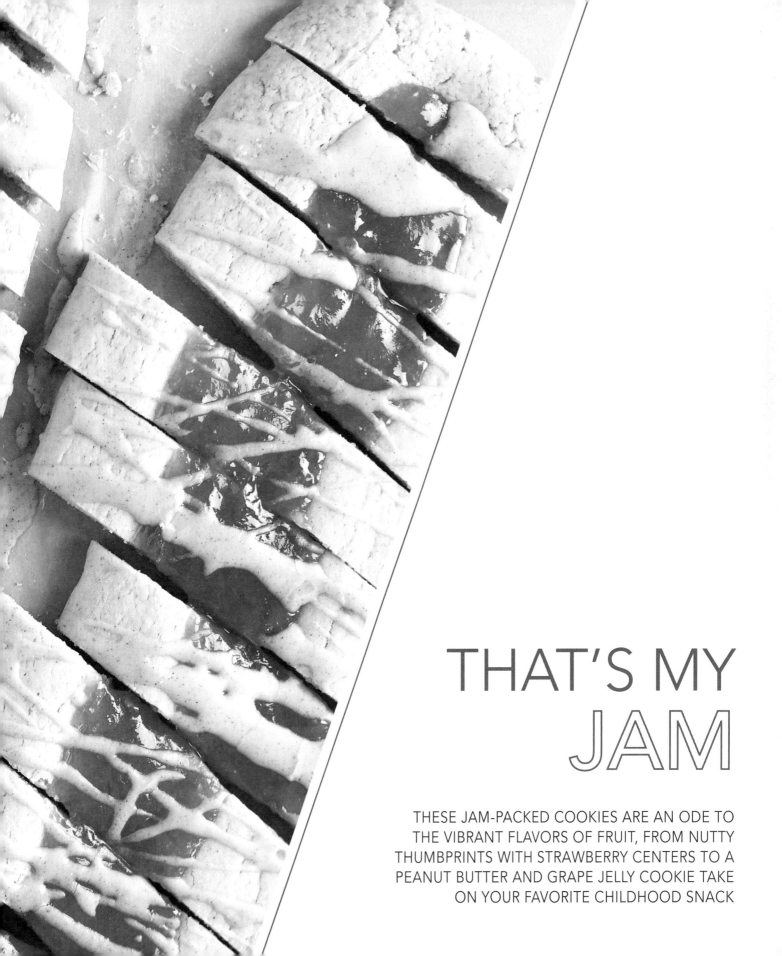

THAT'S MY JAM

THESE JAM-PACKED COOKIES ARE AN ODE TO
THE VIBRANT FLAVORS OF FRUIT, FROM NUTTY
THUMBPRINTS WITH STRAWBERRY CENTERS TO A
PEANUT BUTTER AND GRAPE JELLY COOKIE TAKE
ON YOUR FAVORITE CHILDHOOD SNACK

FINNISH PINWHEEL COOKIES (JOULUTORTTU)

Makes about 24 cookies

Walking the fine line between a cookie and a tart, the joulutorttu is a favorite holiday treat found in bakeries and homes across Finland. The traditional recipe calls for a prune preserve filling, but we opted for a bright, boozy cranberry and ruby port reduction.

3   cups (375 grams) all-purpose flour
1   cup (227 grams) cold unsalted butter, cubed
1   teaspoon (3 grams) kosher salt
1   cup (225 grams) ricotta cheese
¼   cup (60 grams) whole milk
Cranberry Port Preserves (recipe follows)
Garnish: confectioners' sugar

1. In the work bowl of a food processor, place flour, cold butter, and salt; pulse until mixture is crumbly. Add ricotta and milk, and pulse until dough comes together. Divide dough into 3 equal portions. Shape each portion into a disk, and wrap in plastic wrap. Refrigerate overnight.
2. Preheat oven to 400°F (200°C). Line 3 rimmed baking sheets with parchment paper.
3. Working with one disk of dough at a time, roll dough to ⅛-inch thickness on a lightly floured surface. Using a 3-inch square cutter, cut dough, and place on prepared pans. On each square, make 4 (1-inch) cuts at corners diagonally toward center. Place 1 teaspoon (7 grams) Cranberry Port Preserves in center of each cookie. Fold every other tip over toward center, forming a pinwheel. Dab ends of tips with water to help adhere and prevent separation during baking.
4. Bake until edges are just barely golden brown, 11 to 12 minutes. Let cool completely on pans. Dust with confectioners' sugar, if desired.

CRANBERRY PORT PRESERVES
Makes about 1 cup

2   cups (210 grams) frozen cranberries, thawed
¼   cup (55 grams) firmly packed light brown sugar
¼   cup (60 grams) water
¼   cup (60 grams) ruby port wine

1. In a medium saucepan, bring all ingredients to a boil over medium-high heat. Mash cranberries, and reduce heat to low; simmer for 10 minutes. Pour mixture into a jar with a tight-fitting lid, and let cool completely. Refrigerate any leftover cranberry preserves for up to 2 weeks. (Leftover hot preserves can be transferred to sterilized jars, water bath processed for 10 minutes, and stored for up to 6 months.)

JAM-FILLED PECAN SNOWBALLS

Makes 25 cookies

Recipe by Edd Kimber

These classic snowballs are a wonderful thing, especially if you like to entertain or have family visiting. They can be quickly whipped up in a food processor and made in big batches.

1   cup (100 grams) pecan halves
1   cup (227 grams) unsalted butter, softened
⅔   cup (80 grams) confectioners' sugar, plus more for coating
1   teaspoon (4 grams) vanilla extract
2¼ cups (281 grams) all-purpose flour
1   teaspoon (2 grams) ground cinnamon
½   teaspoon (2.5 grams) baking soda
½   teaspoon (1.5 grams) kosher salt
½   cup (160 grams) raspberry jam

1. Preheat oven to 350°F (180°C).
2. Place pecans on a quarter sheet pan, and toast until fragrant and slightly darkened, 8 to 10 minutes. Let cool completely.
3. In the work bowl of a food processor, place toasted pecans; pulse until finely chopped. Transfer to a bowl, and set aside.
4. Place butter, confectioners' sugar, and vanilla in food processor; pulse until well combined and butter is pale and creamy. Add pecans, flour, cinnamon, baking soda, and salt; pulse until a dough forms. Scrape dough into a bowl, and cover with plastic wrap. Refrigerate until firm.
5. Line 2 half sheet pans with parchment paper.
6. Roll dough into 2-tablespoon balls (about 27 grams each). Using a sharp knife, cut each ball in half. Using a finger, make an indentation in center of cut side of each half. Spoon about 1 teaspoon (7 grams) jam into one half. Place second half back on top, and gently smooth seal to join 2 halves back together. Place about 1 inch apart on prepared pans. Refrigerate for 20 minutes.
7. Bake until edges are lightly browned, 15 to 17 minutes. Let cool for 3 minutes; carefully roll in confectioners' sugar to coat. (This has to be done while warm so sugar sticks to the cookies.) Store in an airtight container for up to 4 days.

Photo by Edd Kimber

JAMARETTI COOKIES

Makes about 26 cookies

Recipe by Laura Kasavan

These cookies are a hybrid of two classics: Italian amaretti and traditional American thumbprint cookies. The amaretto is an almond-flavored macaron native to Saronno in Northern Italy. Fragrant with almond paste and filled with sweet apricot jam, the Jamaretti Cookies are finished with a drizzle of Cinnamon Cardamom Glaze.

2¼   cups (281 grams) all-purpose flour
1   teaspoon (5 grams) baking powder
½   teaspoon (1.5 grams) kosher salt
½   teaspoon (1 gram) ground cinnamon
4   ounces (118 grams) almond paste, cubed
¾   cup (150 grams) granulated sugar
½   cup (113 grams) unsalted butter, cubed and softened
2   large eggs (100 grams), room temperature
½   teaspoon (2 grams) almond extract
⅔   cup (213 grams) apricot jam
Cinnamon Cardamom Glaze (recipe follows)

1. In a medium bowl, whisk together flour, baking powder, salt, and cinnamon. Set aside.
2. In the work bowl of a food processor, place almond paste and sugar; process until combined. Add butter, eggs, and almond extract, and process until smooth. Add flour mixture, and process just until a soft dough forms, no more than 30 seconds. Using a bench scraper, divide dough in half, and turn out onto 2 pieces of plastic wrap. (Dough will be sticky.) Shape each half into a disk, and wrap in plastic wrap. Refrigerate for at least 1 hour.
3. Preheat oven to 350°F (180°C). Line a rimmed baking sheet with parchment paper.
4. On a lightly floured surface, shape each disk of dough into 2 (14x3-inch) logs; place on prepared pan.

5. Bake just until set, about 15 minutes. Remove from oven, and make an indentation down center of each log using the back of a tablespoon. In a small microwave-safe bowl, microwave jam for 10 seconds. Stir jam to loosen; fill center of each log with jam. Bake until golden, 12 to 14 minutes more. Let cool completely on a wire rack.
6. Drizzle Cinnamon Cardamom Glaze over cooled cookies. Let stand until set, about 30 minutes. Using a serrated knife, cut logs diagonally into slices.

CINNAMON CARDAMOM GLAZE
Makes about ½ cup

¾   cup (90 grams) confectioners' sugar, sifted
2   tablespoons (30 grams) whole milk
½   tablespoon (7 grams) unsalted butter, melted
1   teaspoon (4 grams) vanilla extract
¼   teaspoon ground cinnamon
⅛   teaspoon kosher salt
⅛   teaspoon ground cardamom

1. In a small bowl, whisk together all ingredients until smooth. Use immediately.

Photo by Laura Kasavan

SOUR CHERRY SHORTBREAD LINZER COOKIES

Makes 12 sandwich cookies

These are the best sandwich cookies you'll make during the summer. A tiny bit of citric acid in the cookie dough creates a zesty sour cherry flavor, which balances out the buttery notes in these shortbread cookies.

¾   cup (170 grams) unsalted butter, softened
½   cup (60 grams) confectioners' sugar
¼   teaspoon (1 gram) vanilla extract
1½ cups (188 grams) all-purpose flour
½   teaspoon (1.5 grams) citric acid
¼   teaspoon kosher salt
2   tablespoons (24 grams) granulated sugar
¼   cup (80 grams) cherry preserves

1. In the bowl of a stand mixer fitted with the paddle attachment, beat butter, confectioners' sugar, and vanilla at medium speed until creamy, 2 to 3 minutes, stopping to scrape sides of bowl.
2. In a medium bowl, sift together flour, citric acid, and salt. With mixer on low speed, gradually add flour mixture to butter mixture, beating until combined. Divide dough in half, and wrap in plastic wrap. Refrigerate for at least 2 hours or overnight.
3. Preheat oven to 350°F (180°C). Line 2 baking sheets with parchment paper.
4. On a lightly floured surface, roll half of dough to ⅛-inch thickness. Using a 2½-inch fluted round cutter, cut dough, rerolling scraps only once. Repeat with remaining dough. Using a 1-inch fluted round cutter, cut centers from half of cookies. Place 1 inch apart on prepared pans. Sprinkle with granulated sugar.
5. Bake until just set, 8 to 10 minutes. (Be careful not to overbake, or cookies will look speckled.) Let cool completely on pans. Spread about 1 teaspoon (7 grams) cherry preserves onto flat side of all solid cookies. Place cookies with cutouts, flat side down, on top of preserves. Bake 2 minutes more. Let cool completely. Store in an airtight container at room temperature for up to 5 days.

Makes about 30 sandwich cookies

Recipe by Jenn Yee

These sandwich cookies are perfect for brunches, teas, and showers. The tangy lemon curd pairs beautifully with the lavender. Prepare this recipe over the course of two days to break up the workload and ensure the dough and curd are well-chilled before baking.

¾   cup (170 grams) unsalted butter, softened
½   cup plus 2 tablespoons (124 grams) granulated sugar
1   teaspoon (2 grams) dried culinary lavender, coarsely ground or finely chopped
1   large egg yolk (19 grams)
1   teaspoon (4 grams) pure vanilla extract
2   cups (250 grams) all-purpose flour
¾   teaspoon (2.25 grams) kosher salt
Confectioners' sugar, for dusting
Lemon Curd Filling (recipe follows)

1. In the bowl of a stand mixer fitted with the paddle attachment, beat butter, granulated sugar, and lavender at medium speed until creamy, 3 to 4 minutes, stopping to scrape sides of bowl. With mixer on low speed, add egg yolk and vanilla, beating just until incorporated, 15 to 30 seconds. (It may not be completely combined, but we want to avoid overwhipping the eggs, which can make for uneven cookies.) Once again, scrape sides of bowl.
2. In a medium bowl, whisk together flour and salt. Gradually add flour mixture to butter mixture, beating just until combined. Scrape sides of bowl, and incorporate any remaining flour.
3. On your work surface, divide dough in half, and shape each half into a disk. The warmth from your hands will help the dough come together. Wrap in plastic wrap, and refrigerate until firm, at least 3 hours. I leave it overnight, and resume the process the next day.
4. Preheat oven to 350°F (180°C). Line rimmed baking sheets with parchment paper.
5. Unwrap one disk of dough, and roll to ¼-inch thickness. If dough is too firm, let it sit out until it is pliable but still cold. If dough is too soft and starts sticking while rolling, place it on a parchment-lined sheet pan, and place it in the refrigerator for 5 to 10 minutes before continuing to roll it out.
6. Using a 2¼-inch fluted round cutter, cut dough, rerolling scraps as necessary. Using a ¾-inch round cutter or piping tip, cut centers from half of cookies. Use a wooden pick to remove dough from piping tip. Place cookies 1 inch apart on prepared pans. They shouldn't spread in the oven. Repeat with remaining dough. You should end up with about 30 cookie tops with centers cut out and about 30 cookie bottoms.
7. Bake each tray in middle rack of the oven until cookies are golden on the edges, 8 to 10 minutes, rotating pans halfway through baking. Let cool on pans for 5 minutes. Remove from pans, and let cool completely on wire racks.

LAVENDER SANDWICH COOKIES WITH LEMON CURD FILLING

8. To assemble, place cookie tops on a sheet pan. Dust with confectioners' sugar. Turn cookie bottoms over so they are bottom side up. Spoon 1½ teaspoons Lemon Curd Filling in center of each, leaving a ½-inch border. Be careful not to put too much or else it will splurt out when you sandwich them. You can also fill a piping bag fitted with a small round tip, and quickly pipe the filling in the center of each cookie. This is best done with cold hands to prevent the curd from warming up. Gently place powdered cookies on top of curd, and press slightly to sandwich them. Serve immediately.

Lemon Curd Filling
Makes 1 cup

½   cup (100 grams) granulated sugar
1   tablespoon (8 grams) cornstarch
¼   teaspoon kosher salt
½   cup (120 grams) fresh lemon juice (from 3 to 4 lemons)
2   large eggs (100 grams)
2   large egg yolks (37 grams)
1   tablespoon (6 grams) finely grated lemon zest
¼   cup (57 grams) cold unsalted butter, cubed

1. Place a fine-mesh sieve over a medium bowl, and set aside.
2. In another medium bowl, whisk together sugar, cornstarch, and salt. Gradually add lemon juice, and whisk until cornstarch dissolves completely. Add eggs and egg yolks, and whisk until well combined.
3. Set the bowl over a saucepan of simmering water, making sure the bottom of the bowl does not touch the water. Cook, whisking constantly, until mixture begins to thicken, 3 to 4 minutes. Then whisk vigorously for 1 minute more. It should have a pudding-like consistency. Remove the bowl from the pot of simmering water.
4. Press curd through sieve. Whisk in zest and butter, 1 to 2 pieces at a time, letting the cubes melt before adding additional butter. Let curd cool to room temperature.
5. Once cool, press a piece of plastic wrap directly against surface of lemon curd to prevent a skin from forming, and refrigerate until well chilled and set, at least 6 hours

Photo by Kassie Borreson

ROSEMARY SHORTBREAD SANDWICH COOKIES WITH CONCORD GRAPE JAM

Makes about 12 sandwich cookies

Recipe by Laura Kasavan

Buttery shortbread rounds infused with rosemary offer a lovely, herbaceous counterpoint to Concord Grape Jam. A final sprinkle of granulated sugar makes these sandwich cookies sparkle.

¾   cup (170 grams) unsalted butter, softened
⅔   cup (133 grams) plus 2 tablespoons
        (24 grams) granulated sugar, divided
½   teaspoon finely chopped fresh rosemary
½   teaspoon (2 grams) vanilla extract
⅛   teaspoon kosher salt
1¾ cups (219 grams) all-purpose flour
Fresh rosemary leaves (optional)
Concord Grape Jam (recipe follows)

1. In the bowl of a stand mixer fitted with the paddle attachment, beat butter, ⅔ cup (133 grams) sugar, and chopped rosemary at medium speed until creamy, 3 to 4 minutes, stopping to scrape sides of bowl. With mixer on medium-low speed, add vanilla and salt, beating until combined. With mixer on low speed, add flour, beating until combined and dough starts to come together. Turn out dough, and shape into a disk. Wrap tightly in plastic wrap, and refrigerate until firm, about 45 minutes.
2. Preheat oven to 350°F (180°C). Line 2 baking sheets with parchment paper.
3. On a lightly floured surface, roll dough to ¼-inch thickness. Using a 2-inch fluted round cutter dipped in flour, cut dough, rerolling scraps as necessary. Place on prepared pans, and sprinkle with remaining 2 tablespoons (24 grams) sugar. Top half of cookies with rosemary leaves, if desired. Refrigerate for 20 minutes.
4. Bake until lightly golden and tops and edges are set, 14 to 16 minutes, rotating pans halfway through baking. Let cool on pans for 5 minutes. Remove from pans, and let cool completely on wire racks.
5. Place a spoonful of Concord Grape Jam on flat side of plain cookies. Place rosemary-topped cookies, flat side down, on top of jam.

CONCORD GRAPE JAM
Makes about ½ cup

2   cups (300 grams) Concord grapes
½   cup (100 grams) granulated sugar
1½ tablespoons (22.5 grams) water, divided
⅛   teaspoon kosher salt
1½ teaspoons (4.5 grams) cornstarch

1. In a medium saucepan, bring Concord grapes, sugar, 1 tablespoon (15 grams) water, and salt to a boil over medium heat. Reduce heat to low, and simmer for 10 minutes. Press mixture through a fine-mesh sieve into a bowl; discard solids. Return mixture to saucepan.
2. In a small bowl, stir together cornstarch and remaining ½ tablespoon (7.5 grams) water. Add cornstarch mixture to saucepan. Simmer, stirring constantly, until mixture is slightly thickened, about 3 minutes. Remove from heat; let cool before using. Pour mixture into a glass bowl, and let cool before using.

Photo by Laura Kasavan

PRO TIP
If fresh Concord grapes are not available, you can substitute high-quality store-bought Concord grape jam for the homemade jam. We suggest using Stonewall Kitchen Concord Grape Jelly, available at *stonewallkitchen.com*.

NUTTY THUMBPRINT COOKIES WITH JAM

Makes about 36 cookies

This cookie is well-balanced: slightly sweet, lightly salted, and chock-full of nuts. The jam center seals the deal. Each one is a bite of perfection.

1   cup (100 grams) walnut halves
1   cup (100 grams) pecan halves
1   teaspoon (3 grams) kosher salt, divided
1   teaspoon grated fresh nutmeg, divided
1   cup (227 grams) unsalted butter, softened
⅔   cup (133 grams) granulated sugar
2   large egg yolks (37 grams)
½   teaspoon (3 grams) vanilla bean paste
2¼   cups (281 grams) all-purpose flour
¾   cup (240 grams) Quick Strawberry Jam or
     Quick Blackberry-Blueberry Jam (recipes follow)

1. Preheat oven to 350°F (180°C). Line baking sheets with parchment paper.
2. In the work bowl of a food processor, pulse together walnuts, pecans, ½ teaspoon (1.5 grams) salt, and ½ teaspoon nutmeg until combined and nuts are finely ground, about 30 seconds. Transfer mixture to a small bowl, and set aside.
3. In the bowl of a stand mixer fitted with the paddle attachment, beat butter and sugar at medium-high speed until creamy, 3 to 4 minutes, stopping to scrape sides of bowl. Reduce mixer speed to medium. Add egg yolks and vanilla bean paste, beating to combine. Reduce mixer speed to low. Add flour, ¾ cup chopped nut mixture, remaining ½ teaspoon (1.5 grams) salt, and remaining ½ teaspoon nutmeg. Increase mixer speed to medium, and beat just until mixture comes together, 2 to 3 minutes.
4. Roll dough into 1-inch balls. Roll balls in remaining nut mixture to coat, and place 2 inches apart on prepared pans. Using your thumb or the back of a spoon, gently make an indentation in center of each ball.
5. Bake for 10 minutes; remove from oven, and press down centers again. Fill centers of cookies with desired jam. Bake until lightly browned, 3 to 5 minutes more. Let cool on pans for 2 minutes. Remove from pans, and let cool completely on wire racks.

QUICK STRAWBERRY JAM
Makes 2 cups

1   pound (455 grams) fresh strawberries, hulled and chopped
1¼   cups (250 grams) granulated sugar
1   lemon (99 grams), juiced

1. In a medium saucepan, bring all ingredients to a boil over medium-high heat. Cook for 5 minutes, stirring frequently. Reduce heat to medium-low; cook, stirring frequently and mashing berries with a potato masher, until mixture thickens, 20 to 45 minutes. (See Note.)
2. Remove from heat; let cool for 30 minutes. Transfer to a clean jar. Jam will keep refrigerated for up to 2 weeks.

QUICK BLACKBERRY-BLUEBERRY JAM
Makes 2 cups

½   pound (225 grams) fresh blackberries
½   pound (225 grams) fresh blueberries
2   cups (400 grams) granulated sugar
1 lemon (99 grams), juiced

1. In a large saucepan, stir together all ingredients with a wooden spoon until combined. Let stand for 2 hours.
2. Bring mixture to a boil over medium-high heat. Cook for 5 minutes, stirring frequently. Reduce heat to medium; cook, stirring frequently and mashing berries with a potato masher, until mixture thickens, 20 to 45 minutes. (See Note.)
3. Remove from heat; let cool for 1 hour. Transfer to a clean jar. Jam will keep refrigerated for up to 2 weeks.

Note: *The ripeness of berries can affect the cook time of jam. This jam could take anywhere from 20 minutes for very ripe berries to 45 minutes for less-ripe berries. To test your jam for doneness, scrape the bottom of the saucepan with your spoon—if the jam parts for a few seconds, it is ready.*

PEANUT BUTTER AND JELLY SANDWICH COOKIES

Makes 14 sandwich cookies

For this decadent sandwich cookie, we layered creamy Peanut Butter Mousse and tart grape jelly between two pillowy peanut butter cookies. Grape jelly is our go-to, but you'll still get delicious results with any variety.

½ cup (113 grams) unsalted butter, softened
1 cup (200 grams) granulated sugar, divided
½ cup (110 grams) firmly packed light brown sugar
1 large egg (50 grams)
1 large egg yolk (19 grams)
¾ cup (192 grams) creamy peanut butter*
2 teaspoons (12 grams) vanilla bean paste
1½ cups (188 grams) all-purpose flour
½ teaspoon (2.5 grams) baking powder
½ teaspoon (2.5 grams) baking soda
¼ teaspoon kosher salt
Peanut Butter Mousse (recipe follows)
⅓ cup (107 grams) grape jelly

1. Line a baking sheet with parchment paper.
2. In the bowl of a stand mixer fitted with the paddle attachment, beat butter, ½ cup (100 grams) granulated sugar, and brown sugar at medium speed until fluffy, 2 to 3 minutes, stopping to scrape sides of bowl. Add egg and egg yolk, beating well. Add peanut butter and vanilla bean paste, beating until combined.
3. In a medium bowl, whisk together flour, baking powder, baking soda, and salt. With mixer on low speed, gradually add flour mixture to butter mixture, beating just until combined. Using a 1½-tablespoon spring-loaded scoop, scoop dough into mounds (about 28 grams each), and place on prepared pan. Refrigerate for 30 minutes.
4. Preheat oven to 350°F (180°C). Line 2 baking sheets with parchment paper.
5. Place remaining ½ cup (100 grams) granulated sugar in a small bowl. Roll each mound into a ball, and roll balls in sugar, coating completely. Place 2½ inches apart on prepared pans. Press tines of a fork into each ball, making a crosshatch design.

6. Bake until light golden brown, 10 to 12 minutes, rotating pans halfway through baking. Let cool on pans for 5 minutes. Remove from pans, and let cool completely on wire racks.
7. Place Peanut Butter Mousse in a piping bag fitted with a ½-inch round piping tip (Ateco #805). Pipe Peanut Butter Mousse onto flat side of half of cookies. Spoon about 1 teaspoon (7 grams) jelly onto flat side of remaining cookies. Sandwich together peanut butter cookies and jelly cookies. Refrigerate until filling is set, about 30 minutes. Cover and refrigerate for up to 3 days.

We used JIF Natural Creamy Peanut Butter.

PEANUT BUTTER MOUSSE
Makes about 2 cups

½ cup (113 grams) unsalted butter, softened
4 ounces (115 grams) cream cheese, softened
⅓ cup (85 grams) creamy peanut butter*
¾ cup (90 grams) confectioners' sugar
1 tablespoon (15 grams) heavy whipping cream

1. In the bowl of a stand mixer fitted with the paddle attachment, beat butter and cream cheese at medium speed until smooth. Beat in peanut butter. Gradually add confectioners' sugar in two additions alternately with cream, beating until smooth. Use immediately.

We used JIF Natural Creamy Peanut Butter.

SHORTBREAD LINZER COOKIES WITH RASPBERRY JAM FILLING

Makes about 18 sandwich cookies

Recipe by Erin Clarkson

Crossing a traditional shortbread recipe with a bright raspberry filling, these sandwich cookies are a buttery revamp on the Linzer-style cookie.

¾ cup (170 grams) unsalted butter, softened
½ cup plus 1 tablespoon (67 grams) confectioners' sugar, sifted
1 teaspoon (6 grams) vanilla bean paste
¼ teaspoon kosher salt
2⅛ cups (265 grams) all-purpose flour
Raspberry Jam Filling (recipe follows)
Garnish: confectioners' sugar

1. In the bowl of a stand mixer fitted with the paddle attachment, beat butter, confectioners' sugar, vanilla bean paste, and salt at medium speed until creamy, 2 to 3 minutes, stopping to scrape sides of bowl. Add flour, and beat at low speed just until combined. Turn out dough, and shape into a disk. Wrap tightly in plastic wrap, and refrigerate for at least 2 hours or overnight.
2. Let dough stand at room temperature until slightly softened, 10 to 15 minutes. Cut 2 (18x13-inch) sheets of parchment paper. Turn out dough onto 1 sheet of parchment, and flatten into a rough rectangle. Top with second sheet of parchment, smoothing down well. Roll to ¼-inch thickness. (Remove top sheet, and smooth down again if you are getting wrinkles.) Transfer dough between parchment to a half sheet pan. Freeze for 15 to 20 minutes.
3. Preheat oven to 325°F (170°C). Line 2 baking sheets with parchment paper.
4. Remove dough from freezer, and remove top sheet of parchment. Using a 2-inch fluted round cutter, cut dough, and place 2 inches apart on prepared pans. If at any point your dough gets difficult to work with or gets too soft, place in freezer again for 5 minutes to firm up. Reroll any scraps, refreeze, and cut out more rounds. Freeze for 10 minutes. Using desired small holiday-shaped cutters, cut centers from half of cookies.
5. Bake, one batch at a time, until set and just beginning to turn golden, 11 to 12 minutes. Let cool on pans for 15 minutes. Remove from pans, and let cool completely on wire racks.

6. Pipe or spoon about 1 teaspoon Raspberry Jam Filling onto flat side of all solid cookies. Generously dust cookies with cutouts with confectioners' sugar, if desired. Place cookies with cutouts, flat side down, on top of filling. Store in an airtight container. If you are not planning on eating these on the first or second day, store cookies and filling separately, and sandwich before eating to avoid them getting soggy.

Note: *Freeze dough you are not working with or cookies that are waiting to bake until ready to use.*

RASPBERRY JAM FILLING
Makes about 2 cups

2 cups (342 grams) frozen raspberries
2 cups (400 grams) granulated sugar

1. In a medium heavy-bottomed saucepan, mash raspberries roughly. Bring to a rolling boil; add sugar, and cook for 3 minutes, stirring occasionally. Transfer to a container or sterilized jars, and let cool completely. Refrigerate overnight before using.

Note: *This will make a little more than you need, but it is perfect as the filling for a cake or for your morning toast.*

Photo by Erin Clarkson

BETTER
WITH
BUTTER

HIGH BUTTER CONTENT GIVES THESE COOKIES INCREDIBLE TEXTURE AND FLAVOR, FROM ZESTY SABLÉS TO MELT-IN-YOUR-MOUTH SHORTBREAD AND EVERY CRUMBLY COOKIE IN BETWEEN

STRAWBERRY AND ROSEMARY SHORTBREAD

Makes 8 to 10 servings

This herbal, crumbly shortbread turns a blush pink with a final dusting of Strawberry Sugar.

1   cup (227 grams) unsalted butter, softened
½   cup (100 grams) granulated sugar
1½   cups (188 grams) all-purpose flour
½   cup (64 grams) cornstarch
⅓   cup (5 grams) freeze-dried strawberries, powdered (see PRO TIP)
½   teaspoon (1.5 grams) kosher salt
1   tablespoon (2 grams) chopped fresh rosemary
⅓   cup (49 grams) diced fresh strawberries
Strawberry Sugar (recipe follows)

1. Preheat oven to 350°F (180°C). Butter and flour a 9-inch square baking dish.
2. In the bowl of a stand mixer fitted with the paddle attachment, beat butter and granulated sugar at medium speed until creamy, 3 to 4 minutes, stopping to scrape sides of bowl.
3. In a medium bowl, sift together flour, cornstarch, freeze-dried strawberries, and salt. Stir in rosemary. With mixer on low speed, gradually add flour mixture to butter mixture, beating until almost combined. Add fresh strawberries, beating until combined.
4. Turn out dough onto a heavily floured surface. Using well-floured hands, knead dough 5 to 10 times, about 1 minute. Press dough into prepared pan.
5. Bake until lightly golden, 30 to 35 minutes. Let cool completely on a wire rack. Sprinkle with Strawberry Sugar.

STRAWBERRY SUGAR

Makes about ½ cup

½   cup (8 grams) freeze-dried strawberries
⅓   cup (67 grams) granulated sugar

1. In the work bowl of a food processor, place freeze-dried strawberries and sugar; process until a fine pink sugar forms, about 2 minutes.

PRO TIP
To make powdered freeze-dried strawberries, place freeze-dried strawberries in the bowl of a food processor; pulse until reduced to a powder.

CARAMELIZED WHITE CHOCOLATE SABLÉS WITH SEA SALT

Makes about 48 cookies

Recipe by Zoë François

White chocolate often leaves me wanting more flavor, so caramelizing it before adding it to the cookie batter gives it the toasty notes of butterscotch with the richness of chocolate. It may go through an awkward phase as you caramelize it, but don't worry, it'll turn into a golden delight by the end.

1½ cups (255 grams) chopped white chocolate
1 cup (227 grams) unsalted butter, softened
¾ cup (150 grams) granulated sugar
1 large egg yolk (19 grams)
1 teaspoon (4 grams) vanilla extract
2 cups (250 grams) all-purpose flour
¼ teaspoon kosher salt
3 to 4 tablespoons (45 to 60 grams) heavy whipping cream, warmed
Sea salt, for sprinkling

1. Preheat oven to 300°F (150°C). Line a baking sheet with a nonstick baking mat.
2. Spread white chocolate on prepared pan.
3. Bake until chocolate starts to melt, about 10 minutes. Using a spatula, spread chocolate into a thin layer. Bake 10 minutes more. Stir, and repeat procedure until chocolate is caramel colored. The chocolate may liquefy, or it may become granular. If chocolate is grainy, place it in a coffee grinder or blender to smooth it out. It doesn't need to be perfectly smooth at this point. Let cool slightly. If you make this ahead, warm it slightly in microwave for 10 to 20 seconds before proceeding.
4. In the bowl of a stand mixer fitted with the paddle attachment, beat butter and sugar at medium speed until creamy, 2 to 3 minutes, stopping to scrape sides of bowl. Add egg yolk and vanilla, and beat for 1 minute. Add 3 tablespoons (57 grams) softened caramelized white chocolate, beating until combined. With mixer on low speed, gradually add flour and kosher salt, beating just until combined.

5. Divide dough in half, and shape each half into a 1½-inch-wide log. Wrap logs in plastic wrap, and refrigerate for at least 1 hour or overnight.
6. Preheat oven to 350°F (180°C). Line a baking sheet with parchment paper.
7. Cut logs into ¼-inch-thick slices, and place on prepared pan.
8. Bake until edges are golden, 8 to 10 minutes. Let cool completely on wire racks.
9. In a microwave-safe bowl, microwave remaining caramelized white chocolate to soften. Add warm cream, 1 teaspoon (5 grams) at a time, stirring until white chocolate is thin enough to spread but not too liquidy. Spread 1 teaspoon ganache onto each cookie, and sprinkle with sea salt. Serve the same day, or cookies will soften.

Photo by Zoë François

DANISH BUTTER COOKIES

Makes 15 to 20 cookies

Recipe by Joshua Weissman

This is a homemade rendition of the classic Royal Dansk cookies. The crisp cookies come in all sorts of shapes and textures in a round blue tin. With a snappy crunch and buttery background flavor, this from-scratch version has even better flavor and richness.

¾   cup plus 1 tablespoon (184 grams) unsalted butter, softened
¾   cup (150 grams) granulated sugar
2   tablespoons (26 grams) vanilla extract
3   large eggs (150 grams), divided
1¾   cups (219 grams) all-purpose flour*
1   teaspoon (3 grams) kosher salt
Edible gold sparkling sugar, for sprinkling

1. In the bowl of a stand mixer fitted with the paddle attachment, beat butter, granulated sugar, and vanilla at medium speed until creamy, 2 to 3 minutes, stopping to scrape sides of bowl. Add 2 eggs (100 grams), one at a time, beating well after each addition.
2. With mixer on low speed, gradually add flour and salt, beating until a cohesive dough forms. Turn out dough, and use a bench scraper to divide into thirds. Shape each piece into a disk, and wrap in plastic wrap. Refrigerate until firm, about 2½ hours.
3. Preheat oven to 350°F (180°C). Line baking sheets with parchment paper.
4. Remove one disk of dough from refrigerator, and let stand at room temperature until slightly softened, about 5 minutes. Between 2 sheets of lightly floured parchment paper, roll dough to ¼-inch thickness. Remove top sheet of parchment. Using a 2¾-inch fluted round cutter, cut dough, and place on prepared pans. Using a 1-inch round cutter, cut centers from cookies. Repeat with remaining dough.
5. In a small bowl, lightly whisk remaining 1 egg (50 grams). Brush egg wash onto dough, and sprinkle with sparkling sugar. Freeze until firm, about 12 minutes.
6. Bake until edges are just beginning to brown, 10 to 15 minutes. Let cool completely on wire racks. Store in an airtight container.

We used Bob's Red Mill All-Purpose Flour.

Photo by Joshua Weissman

ORANGE BUTTER COOKIES

Makes 24 cookies

There are so many things to love about these cookies. The dough doesn't need refrigerating, holds an impressive cookie stamp imprint, and combines citrusy orange with smooth bittersweet chocolate. Bake for 6 minutes for nice soft cookies, or bake a few minutes more for those satisfyingly crisp, golden-brown edges.

1   cup (227 grams) unsalted butter, softened
2   cups (240 grams) confectioners' sugar
1   large egg (50 grams)
2   tablespoons (6 grams) orange zest
1   teaspoon (4 grams) vanilla extract
3   cups (375 grams) all-purpose flour
2   teaspoons (10 grams) baking powder
1   teaspoon (3 grams) kosher salt
1   cup (200 grams) granulated sugar
6   ounces (175 grams) 60% cacao bittersweet chocolate, chopped

1. Preheat oven to 425°F (220°C). Line 2 rimmed baking sheets with parchment paper.
2. In the bowl of a stand mixer fitted with the paddle attachment, beat butter and confectioners' sugar at medium speed until fluffy, 3 to 4 minutes, stopping to scrape sides of bowl. Add egg, zest, and vanilla, beating until combined.
3. In a medium bowl, whisk together flour, baking powder, and salt. With mixer on low speed, gradually add flour mixture to butter mixture, beating until a dough forms.
4. Using a 2-tablespoon scoop, scoop dough, and roll into balls. Roll balls in granulated sugar, coating completely. Place on prepared pans. Using a cookie stamp*, gently press down on dough balls. (Dough should just barely meet edge of cookie stamp.) Cookies should be 2 inches apart on pans.

5. Bake until golden brown, 6 to 8 minutes. Let cool on pans for 2 minutes. Remove from pans, and let cool completely on wire racks.
6. In the top of a double boiler, place chopped chocolate. Cook over simmering water, stirring constantly, until melted. Remove from heat. Dip bottom of each cookie in melted chocolate, gently scraping bottom of cookie along edge of bowl to remove excess. Place on parchment paper, and let stand until chocolate is set. Store in an airtight container for up to 2 weeks.

We used Nordic Ware Geo Cast Cookie Stamps, available at nordicware.com.

CLASSIC SHORTBREAD

Makes 9 cookies

Time to break out your favorite cookie mold. Thanks to this dough's wet nature and soft crumb, it holds shape and design better than any other biscuit on the block. Our Classic Shortbread is crumbly, buttery bliss. You'll never go back to store-bought again.

¾   cup (170 grams) unsalted butter, softened
½   cup (60 grams) confectioners' sugar
1   teaspoon (4 grams) vanilla extract*
½   teaspoon (1.5 grams) kosher salt
1½ cups (188 grams) all-purpose flour
Garnish: confectioners' sugar

1. In the bowl of a stand mixer fitted with the paddle attachment, beat butter at medium speed until creamy, about 1 minute. Add confectioners' sugar, vanilla, and salt; beat until smooth, about 1 minute. With mixer on low speed, gradually add flour, beating until combined. Increase mixer speed to medium, and beat until very light and fluffy, about 5 minutes. Turn out dough onto a sheet of parchment paper, and shape into a 6-inch square. Wrap in parchment, and refrigerate for at least 1 hour or up to 3 days.
2. Let dough stand at room temperature for 30 minutes.
3. Preheat oven to 325°F (170°C).
4. Break dough into small pieces, and begin pressing pieces into bottom of an 8-inch square shortbread baking pan*. (The dough should become very soft as you work with it. This is important because it helps when pressing the dough into the small crevices.) Press remaining dough into an even layer in pan; prick dough all over with a fork.
5. Bake until dough looks dry but edges have not yet begun to turn golden, 20 to 25 minutes. Let cool in pan for 15 minutes. Invert pan onto a cutting board. Hit pan with the palm of your hand until shortbread releases. Using a sharp knife, immediately slice into squares following imprinted lines. Let cool completely. Garnish with confectioners' sugar, if desired. Store in an airtight container at room temperature for up to 1 week.

We used Heilala Vanilla Extract and Nordic Ware Snowflake Shortbread Baking Pan.

Note: *Because of how soft this dough is, it works best when baked in a cookie mold rather than using cookie stamps.*

PIÑÓN MEXICAN WEDDING COOKIES

Makes about 40 cookies

Recipe by Zoë François

The piñones (a.k.a. pine nuts) make this version of the classic Mexican wedding cookie even more decadent than the traditional. They melt in your mouth and are perfect for parties.

1   cup (135 grams) pine nuts, toasted
⅔   cup (80 grams) confectioners' sugar, divided
1   cup (227 grams) unsalted butter, softened
1   teaspoon (4 grams) vanilla extract
2   cups (250 grams) all-purpose flour
½   teaspoon (1 gram) ground cinnamon
¼   teaspoon kosher salt
Garnish: confectioners' sugar

1. Preheat oven to 325°F (170°C). Line 2 baking sheets with parchment paper.
2. In the work bowl of a food processor, process pine nuts and ⅓ cup (40 grams) confectioners' sugar until finely ground.
3. In the bowl of a stand mixer fitted with the paddle attachment, beat butter and remaining ⅓ cup (40 grams) confectioners' sugar at medium speed until creamy, 2 to 3 minutes, stopping to scrape sides of bowl. Beat in vanilla.
4. With mixer on low speed, gradually add nut mixture, flour, cinnamon, and salt, beating just until combined. Using a 1-tablespoon scoop, scoop dough, and roll into balls. Place 1 inch apart on prepared pans. Refrigerate for 15 minutes.
5. Bake until golden on bottom but still pale on top, 12 to 15 minutes. Let cool completely on pans. Dust with confectioners' sugar, if desired. Store in an airtight container for up to 5 days.

Photo by Zoë François

CHOCOLATE COCONUT ALFAJORES

Makes 25 sandwich cookies

Recipe by Edd Kimber

A South American favorite, alfajores feature a thick layer of dulce de leche sandwiched between two crumbly butter cookies sprinkled with coconut flakes. Thanks to the cornstarch, these are especially tender and will melt in your mouth.

2   cups (250 grams) all-purpose flour
⅔   cup (80 grams) confectioners' sugar
5   tablespoons (40 grams) cornstarch, plus more for dusting
¼   teaspoon kosher salt
1   cup (227 grams) cold unsalted butter, cubed
2   large egg yolks (37 grams)
1   teaspoon (4 grams) vanilla extract
⅔   cup (200 grams) dulce de leche
7   ounces (200 grams) dark chocolate, roughly chopped
⅔   cup (56 grams) desiccated coconut

1. In the work bowl of a food processor, place flour, confectioners' sugar, cornstarch, and salt; pulse until combined. Add cold butter, and pulse until mixture resembles coarse meal. Add egg yolks and vanilla, and pulse until mixture comes together and a dough forms. Divide dough in half.
2. On a work surface lightly dusted with cornstarch, roll each portion of dough into a 2-inch-wide log. Wrap in plastic wrap, and refrigerate until firm, about 2 hours.
3. Preheat oven to 350°F (180°C). Line 2 half sheet pans with parchment paper.
4. Using a sharp knife, cut logs into ¼-inch-thick slices. Place about 1 inch apart on prepared pans.
5. Bake until lightly browned around the edges, 10 to 11 minutes. Let cool completely on pans.
6. Place dulce de leche in a piping bag fitted with a small round tip. Pipe a small round of dulce de leche onto half of cookies. Place remaining cookies on top of dulce de leche, gently pressing together until dulce de leche just reaches edges of cookie. Refrigerate cookies while preparing chocolate.

7. In a medium microwave-safe bowl, microwave chocolate on high in 15- to 20-second intervals, stirring between each, until almost fully melted but some small pieces remain visible. Remove bowl from microwave, and stir vigorously until fully melted. (This is the simplest method of tempering chocolate and needs no thermometer.)
8. Dip cookies halfway into melted chocolate, letting excess drip off. Place on a sheet of parchment paper, and sprinkle coconut over melted chocolate while still warm. Let stand until chocolate is set. Store in an airtight container for up to 2 days, but cookies will soften over time.

Photo by Edd Kimber

GERMAN ALMOND CRESCENT COOKIES

Makes 24 cookies

This crumbly, almond-scented cookie is a classic from Germany. We changed the confectioners' sugar dusting to a homemade vanilla sugar, a vanilla bean seed-speckled coating worth the bit of extra effort.

½ cup (100 grams) superfine castor sugar
1 vanilla bean, split lengthwise, seeds scraped and reserved
2 cups (250 grams) all-purpose flour
1 cup (227 grams) cold unsalted butter, cubed
¾ cup (90 grams) confectioners' sugar
¾ cup (72 grams) almond flour
½ teaspoon (1.5 grams) kosher salt

1. In the container of a blender, place castor sugar and half of vanilla bean seeds; blend on high until a fine powder forms, about 10 seconds. Set aside.
2. In the bowl of a stand mixer fitted with the paddle attachment, beat all-purpose flour, cold butter, confectioners' sugar, almond flour, salt, and remaining vanilla bean seeds at medium-low speed until a crumbly dough forms, 3 to 4 minutes. (Mixture will start out dry and crumbly but will come together.) Shape dough into a disk, and wrap in plastic wrap. Refrigerate for 1 hour.
3. Preheat oven to 350°F (180°C). Line 2 baking sheets with parchment paper.
4. Divide dough into 24 (25-gram) balls. Roll dough balls into 4½-inch logs with tapered ends, and bend each one into a crescent shape. Place about 1 inch apart on prepared pans.
5. Bake, one batch at a time, until edges are just beginning to turn golden (not browned), 12 to 15 minutes. Sift vanilla sugar over hot cookies. Let cool completely; dust with vanilla sugar again. Store in an airtight container for up to 3 weeks.

HAZELNUT BUTTER SANDWICH COOKIES

Makes 20 sandwich cookies

Step aside, Nutter Butter cookies. This hazelnut revamp of a classic sandwich cookie comes equipped with our homemade Hazelnut Butter, your new condiment obsession. A dip in dark chocolate and a roll in even more hazelnuts sends this cookie right over the nutty edge.

1   cup (227 grams) unsalted butter, softened
⅓   cup (87 grams) Hazelnut Butter (recipe follows)
½   cup (110 grams) firmly packed dark brown sugar
1   large egg (50 grams)
1½   teaspoons (9 grams) vanilla bean paste
1⅔   cups (208 grams) all-purpose flour
1   teaspoon (5 grams) baking soda
¾   teaspoon (3.75 grams) baking powder
¼   teaspoon kosher salt
1¼   cups (100 grams) old-fashioned oats
¼   cup (28 grams) chopped dry-roasted unsalted hazelnuts
Hazelnut Buttercream (recipe follows)
1   (10-ounce) package (283.8 grams) dark chocolate melting wafers
Garnish: finely chopped roasted hazelnuts

1. In the bowl of a stand mixer fitted with the paddle attachment, beat butter and Hazelnut Butter at medium speed until smooth, about 3 minutes. Add brown sugar, and beat until creamy, 2 to 3 minutes, stopping to scrape sides of bowl. Add egg and vanilla bean paste, and beat at low speed just until combined, about 30 seconds.
2. In a medium bowl, whisk together flour, baking soda, baking powder, and salt. Gradually add flour mixture to butter mixture, beating just until combined. Add oats and hazelnuts, beating just until combined. Shape dough into a disk, and wrap in plastic wrap. Refrigerate until firm, about 2 hours.
3. Preheat oven to 325°F (170°C). Line 2 baking sheets with parchment paper.
4. Between 2 sheets of parchment paper, roll dough to ¼-inch thickness. Transfer dough between parchment to freezer. Freeze until set, about 20 minutes.
5. Using a 2¼-inch round cutter, cut dough, and place 2 inches apart on prepared pans.
6. Bake until golden brown, about 12 minutes, rotating pans halfway through baking. Let cool on pans for 5 minutes. Remove from pans, and let cool completely on wire racks. (While first round of cookies is baking, reroll any scraps between parchment again, freeze until set, and cut out cookies. Reroll scraps a third time, if needed. Keep cut cookies in freezer until ready to bake.)
7. Place Hazelnut Buttercream in a piping bag fitted with a closed star tip (Ateco #855). Pipe Hazelnut Buttercream onto flat side of half of cookies in a spiral starting at center. Place remaining cookies, flat side down, on top of filling. Refrigerate for 15 minutes.

8. In a microwave-safe bowl, heat chocolate on high in 30-second intervals, stirring between each, until melted and smooth. Let cool slightly, 3 to 5 minutes. Line a baking sheet with parchment paper. Place chopped hazelnuts on a plate. Dip half of each cookie in melted chocolate, and roll in hazelnuts, if desired. Place on prepared pan. Let stand until chocolate is set, 8 to 10 minutes. Store in an airtight container at room temperature if unfilled or in refrigerator if filled for up to 3 days.

HAZELNUT BUTTER

Makes ⅔ cup

1¼   cups (178 grams) dry-roasted unsalted hazelnuts
1½   tablespoons (18 grams) granulated sugar
½   teaspoon (1 gram) ground cinnamon
¼   teaspoon kosher salt

1. In the work bowl of a food processor, process hazelnuts until smooth, about 3 minutes. Add sugar, cinnamon, and salt; process until combined, about 30 seconds. Refrigerate in an airtight container for up to 3 weeks.

HAZELNUT BUTTERCREAM

Makes 3½ cups

¾   cup (170 grams) unsalted butter, softened
⅓   cup (87 grams) Hazelnut Butter (recipe precedes)
4½   cups (540 grams) confectioners' sugar
¼   cup (60 grams) heavy whipping cream
¼   teaspoon kosher salt

1. In the bowl of a stand mixer fitted with the paddle attachment, beat butter and Hazelnut Butter at medium speed until smooth, 2 to 3 minutes. With mixer on low speed, gradually add confectioners' sugar alternately with cream, beating until combined. Add salt, and beat until fluffy, about 3 minutes. Use immediately.

CRANBERRY PECAN MAPLE SHORTBREAD

Makes about 30 cookies

Recipe by Rebecca Firth

Calling all one-bowl baking lovers! This little gem is a one-bowl wonder that comes together in a snap, rolls like a dream, and is a real stunner. Although the finished cookies will look different, you could use regular dried cranberries in a pinch.

1	cup (227 grams) unsalted butter, softened
¾	cup (90 grams) confectioners' sugar
2	large eggs (100 grams), room temperature
2	tablespoons (42 grams) pure maple syrup
1½	teaspoons (6 grams) vanilla extract
½	teaspoon (2 grams) maple extract
½	teaspoon (1.5 grams) sea salt
½	teaspoon (1 gram) ground cinnamon
2½	cups (324 grams) all-purpose flour
¼	cup (4 grams) freeze-dried cranberries
3	tablespoons (21 grams) finely chopped toasted pecans

1. In the bowl of a stand mixer fitted with the paddle attachment, beat butter and confectioners' sugar at medium speed until creamy, 2 to 3 minutes, stopping to scrape sides of bowl. Add eggs, one at a time, beating well after each addition. Add maple syrup, extracts, sea salt, and cinnamon, and beat for 1 minute.

2. With mixer on low speed, gradually add flour, beating just until combined, about 1 minute. Using a spatula, scrape sides and bottom of bowl to ensure everything is incorporated. Shape dough into a disk, and wrap tightly in plastic wrap. Refrigerate for 15 minutes. (You want dough chilled but not so cold that it cracks when rolled out. If you refrigerate longer, let come closer to room temperature before rolling.)

3. Line a baking sheet with parchment paper.

4. On a lightly floured surface, roll dough to ¼- to ½-inch thickness. Add more flour as needed, and turn dough 90 degrees after each roll to keep sticking at bay. In the work bowl of a food processor, process freeze-dried cranberries to a fine powder. Sprinkle dough with cranberry powder and pecans. Roll dough one more time, gently pressing cranberries and pecans into dough. Place dough on prepared pan. Freeze for 10 minutes, or refrigerate for 20 minutes.

5. Position oven rack in top third of oven, no less than 6 inches from heat. Preheat oven to 350°F (180°C). Line several baking sheets with parchment paper.

6. Using a 2½x1½-inch fluted rectangle cutter, cut dough, rerolling scraps as necessary. Place on prepared pans. Freeze for 10 minutes, or refrigerate for 20 minutes.

7. Bake for 8 minutes. Let cool on pans for 5 minutes. Remove from pans, and let cool completely on wire racks. Store in an airtight container for up to 5 days.

Photo by Rebecca Firth

PETIT BEURRE

Makes about 18 sandwich cookies

These simple cookies are rich and only slightly sweet. They are delightful on their own, straight from the oven, but a schmear of buttercream, ganache, or Nutella takes them to the next level.

½   cup plus 2 tablespoons (124 grams) granulated sugar
½   cup (113 grams) unsalted butter
⅓   cup (80 grams) water
3   cups (375 grams) all-purpose flour
½   teaspoon (2.5 grams) baking powder
Strawberry Buttercream (recipe follows)

1. In a small saucepan, bring sugar, butter, and ⅓ cup (80 grams) water to a boil over medium heat. Reduce heat to low, and cook just until butter is melted. Remove from heat, and let cool for 20 minutes, stirring occasionally.
2. In a medium bowl, whisk together flour and baking powder. Add sugar mixture, stirring until combined. Knead by hand until smooth. Shape dough into a disk, and wrap in plastic wrap. Refrigerate for at least 3 hours.
3. Preheat oven to 350°F (180°C). Line baking sheets with parchment paper.
4. On a lightly floured surface, roll dough to ¼-inch thickness. Using a 3x2-inch rectangle cutter, cut dough, rerolling scraps as necessary. Place about ½ inch apart on prepared pans. Using a docker or fork, prick dough.
5. Bake until light golden brown, 10 to 12 minutes, rotating pans halfway through baking. Let cool on pans for 10 minutes. Spread Strawberry Buttercream onto flat side of half of cookies. Place remaining cookies, flat side down, on top of buttercream.

STRAWBERRY BUTTERCREAM

Makes about 2 cups

¾   cup (170 grams) unsalted butter, softened
3   cups (360 grams) confectioners' sugar
¼   teaspoon kosher salt
¼   cup (37 grams) minced fresh strawberries

1. In the bowl of a stand mixer fitted with the paddle attachment, beat butter at medium speed until creamy. Gradually add confectioners' sugar and salt, beating until well combined. Add strawberries, and beat until incorporated. Use immediately.

Photo by Stephen DeVries

CHOCOLATE-ORANGE SABLÉS

Makes about 64 cookies

Bursting with complexity and flavor, these sablés are easier to put together than you might think.

Orange dough:
¾ cup (170 grams) unsalted butter, softened
1 cup (120 grams) confectioners' sugar
3 tablespoons (9 grams) orange zest
1 large egg (50 grams)
1 tablespoon (15 grams) fresh orange juice
1½ cups (188 grams) all-purpose flour
1¼ cups (120 grams) almond flour
1 cup (113 grams) chopped roasted salted pistachios
½ teaspoon (1.5 grams) kosher salt

Chocolate dough:
1 cup (227 grams) unsalted butter, softened
1 cup (120 grams) confectioners' sugar
1 tablespoon (15 grams) fresh orange juice
1 teaspoon (4 grams) vanilla extract
1½ cups (188 grams) all-purpose flour
1 cup (113 grams) chopped roasted salted pistachios
½ cup (43 grams) unsweetened cocoa powder
½ teaspoon (1.5 grams) kosher salt
1 cup (200 grams) turbinado sugar

1. For orange dough: In the bowl of a stand mixer fitted with the paddle attachment, beat butter, confectioners' sugar, and zest at medium speed until fluffy, 3 to 4 minutes, stopping to scrape sides of bowl. Add egg and orange juice, beating to combine.
2. In a medium bowl, whisk together flours, pistachios, and salt. With mixer on low speed, gradually add flour mixture to butter mixture, beating just until combined.
3. Line an 8-inch square baking pan with plastic wrap, letting excess extend over sides of pan. Press orange dough into prepared pan. Refrigerate until firm, 30 minutes to 1 hour.

4. For chocolate dough: In the bowl of a stand mixer fitted with the paddle attachment, beat butter, confectioners' sugar, orange juice, and vanilla at medium speed until creamy, 3 to 4 minutes, stopping to scrape sides of bowl.
5. In a medium bowl, whisk together flour, pistachios, cocoa, and salt. With mixer on low speed, gradually add flour mixture to butter mixture, beating just until combined. Spread chocolate dough on top of orange dough, smoothing as much as possible. Cover and refrigerate until firm, at least 2 hours.
6. Preheat oven to 350°F (180°C). Line baking sheets with parchment paper.
7. Using excess plastic wrap as handles, remove dough from pan, and cut into 2x¼ -inch slices. In a shallow dish, place turbinado sugar. Roll edges of dough in sugar to coat. Place at least ½ inch apart on prepared pans.
8. Bake until firm and just beginning to brown at the edges, 10 to 12 minutes. Let cool completely on a wire rack.

Photo by Stephen DeVries

[butter]

LANGUES DE CHAT

Makes about 36 cookies

These piped cookies are delicious on their own, but dip them in Mint Chocolate Ganache, add a sprinkle of turbinado sugar, and we dare you to eat just one.

½ cup (113 grams) unsalted butter, softened
½ cup (100 grams) granulated sugar
½ vanilla bean, split lengthwise, seeds scraped and reserved
3 large egg whites (90 grams), room temperature
1 cup (125 grams) all-purpose flour
½ teaspoon (1.5 grams) kosher salt
Mint Chocolate Ganache (recipe follows)
Garnish: turbinado sugar

1. Preheat oven to 400°F (200°C). Line a baking sheet with parchment paper or a nonstick baking mat.
2. In the bowl of a stand mixer fitted with the paddle attachment, beat butter, granulated sugar, and vanilla bean seeds at medium speed until creamy, 3 to 4 minutes, stopping to scrape sides of bowl. Reduce mixer speed to medium-low. Add egg whites, one at a time, beating well after each addition.
3. In a medium bowl, sift together flour and salt three times. With mixer on low speed, gradually add flour mixture to butter mixture, beating just until combined.
4. Spoon batter into a large piping bag fitted with a medium round tip. Pipe batter onto prepared pans in straight lines about 3 inches long and ½ inch wide.
5. Bake until edges are golden brown, 10 to 12 minutes. Let cool completely. Dip in Mint Chocolate Ganache, and sprinkle with turbinado sugar, if desired.

Mint Chocolate Ganache
Makes about 1 cup

1 cup (170 grams) chopped 60% cacao bittersweet chocolate
¾ cup (180 grams) heavy whipping cream
½ teaspoon (2 grams) peppermint extract

1. Place chopped chocolate in a medium heatproof bowl.
2. In a small saucepan, bring cream and peppermint extract to a simmer over medium-high heat. Remove from heat; pour hot cream mixture over chocolate. Cover and let stand for 5 minutes; stir until chocolate is melted and mixture is smooth. Use immediately.

Photo by Stephen DeVries

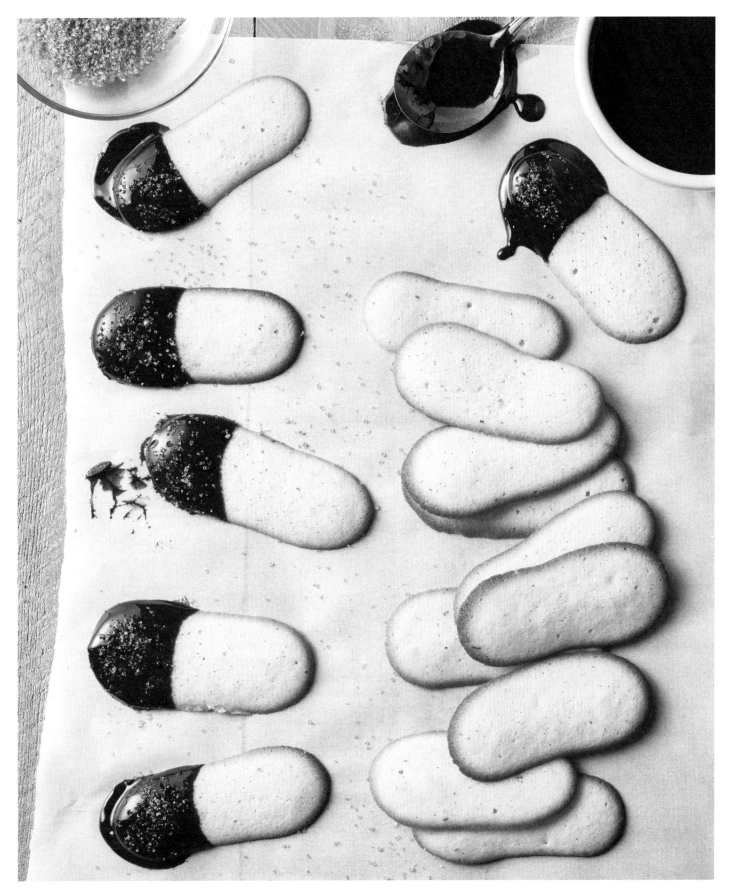

BOOZY
COOKIES

FROM AN IRISH CREAM-FILLED COFFEE
THUMBPRINT TO A CAMPARI AND STRAWBERRY
COOKIE, THESE LIBATION-INSPIRED RECIPES
ARE COCKTAIL HOUR-WORTHY

GLAZED CAMPARI AND STRAWBERRY COOKIES

Makes about 30 cookies

Recipe by Marian Cooper Cairns

If you love a Negroni (the ultimate stiff summer cocktail), this will be your signature summer cookie.

1   cup (227 grams) unsalted butter, softened
1   cup (200 grams) granulated sugar
2   large egg whites (60 grams)
2   tablespoons (30 grams) plus 2 teaspoons (10 grams) heavy whipping cream, divided
1   tablespoon (3 grams) grapefruit zest
1   teaspoon (4 grams) vanilla extract
2¾ cups (344 grams) cake flour
2   teaspoons (10 grams) baking powder
1¼ teaspoons (3.75 grams) kosher salt
1   (0.8-ounce) package (16 grams) freeze-dried strawberries, chopped (about 1 cup)
1 to 1¼ cups (120 to 150 grams) confectioners' sugar
2   tablespoons (30 grams) Campari

1. Preheat oven to 350°F (180°C). Line 2 baking sheets with parchment paper.
2. In the bowl of a stand mixer fitted with the paddle attachment, beat butter and granulated sugar at medium speed until creamy, about 2 minutes, stopping to scrape sides of bowl. Add egg whites, 2 tablespoons (30 grams) cream, zest, and vanilla, beating until well combined.
3. In a medium bowl, stir together flour, baking powder, and salt. With mixer on low speed, gradually add flour mixture to butter mixture, beating just until combined. Stir in freeze-dried strawberries until combined. Using a 2-tablespoon scoop, scoop dough into rounds, and place about 2½ inches apart on prepared pans.
4. Bake until puffed and pale golden, 14 to 16 minutes, rotating pans once. Let cool completely on pans.
5. In a small bowl, whisk together 1 cup (120 grams) confectioners' sugar, Campari, and remaining 2 teaspoons (10 grams) cream until smooth. Add remaining ¼ cup (30 grams) confectioners' sugar, if needed. Dip or drizzle glaze over top of cooled cookies. Let stand until set, about 30 minutes.

Photo by Matt Armendariz

CRÈME FRAÎCHE APRICOT COOKIES

Makes about 24 cookies

This decadent cookie fuses warm and golden brandy, jewel-like dried apricots, crunchy pearl sugar, and a dose of silky crème fraîche.

⅔   cup (85 grams) diced dried apricots
½   cup (120 grams) brandy
⅓   cup (76 grams) unsalted butter, softened
¾   cup (150 grams) granulated sugar
2   large egg yolks (37 grams)
1   large egg (50 grams)
½   cup (120 grams) crème fraîche
2½   cups (313 grams) all-purpose flour
½   teaspoon (2.5 grams) baking powder
¼   teaspoon (1.25 grams) baking soda
¼   teaspoon kosher salt
1   cup (200 grams) pearl sugar*

1. In a small saucepan, bring apricots and brandy just to a boil. Reduce heat, and simmer, stirring occasionally, until almost all liquid is evaporated, 8 to 10 minutes. Remove from heat, and let cool completely.
2. In the bowl of a stand mixer fitted with the paddle attachment, beat butter and granulated sugar at medium speed just until combined, 1 to 2 minutes. Beat in egg yolks and egg. Add crème fraîche, beating until combined.
3. In a medium bowl, whisk together flour, baking powder, baking soda, and salt. With mixer on low speed, gradually add flour mixture to butter mixture, beating until combined. Gently stir in cooled apricots. (Dough will be sticky.) Refrigerate for 30 minutes.
4. Preheat oven to 350°F (180°C). Line 3 rimmed baking sheets with parchment paper.
5. Place pearl sugar in a small bowl. Using a 1½-tablespoon scoop, scoop dough, and roll into balls. (If dough is sticky, you can dampen your hands with water to roll into balls.) Roll balls in pearl sugar, and place 2 inches apart on prepared pans. Flatten slightly with the palm of your hand.
6. Bake, one batch at a time, until cookies are set but not browned, 10 to 12 minutes. Let cool on pans for 5 minutes. Remove from pans, and let cool completely on wire racks.

*We used Lars Own Swedish Pearl Sugar.

SALTED CARAMEL THUMBPRINT COOKIES

Makes about 20 cookies

Recipe by Laura Kasavan

These bourbon-laced thumbprint cookies are rolled in turbinado sugar and filled with Salted Caramel Sauce.

½   cup (57 grams) chopped toasted pecans
⅔   cup (133 grams) granulated sugar
¾   cup (170 grams) unsalted butter, softened
2   tablespoons (30 grams) bourbon
½   teaspoon (2 grams) vanilla extract
⅛   teaspoon kosher salt
1¾   cups (219 grams) all-purpose flour
¼   cup (50 grams) turbinado sugar
Salted Caramel Sauce (recipe follows)
Garnish: flaked sea salt

1. In the work bowl of a food processor, place pecans and granulated sugar; process until combined.
2. In the bowl of a stand mixer fitted with the paddle attachment, beat pecan sugar and butter at medium speed until fluffy, 2 to 3 minutes, stopping to scrape sides of bowl. With mixer on medium-low speed, add bourbon, vanilla, and kosher salt, beating until combined. With mixer on low speed, add flour, beating until combined and dough starts to come together. Turn out dough, and shape into a disk. Wrap tightly in plastic wrap, and refrigerate until firm, about 2 hours.
3. Preheat oven to 350°F (180°C). Line 2 rimmed baking sheets with parchment paper.
4. Place turbinado sugar in a shallow bowl. Shape dough into 1¼-inch balls, and roll in sugar to coat. Place on prepared pans. Freeze for 15 minutes. Using your thumb or the back of a spoon, gently make an indentation in center of each ball.
5. Bake until lightly golden and tops and edges are set, 14 to 16 minutes, rotating pans halfway through baking. Remove from oven, and press down centers again. Let cool on pans for 10 minutes. Remove from pans, and let cool completely on wire racks.
6. Pipe or spoon about 1 teaspoon Salted Caramel Sauce in center of each cookie. Garnish with sea salt, if desired.

SALTED CARAMEL SAUCE
Makes about 1 cup

1   cup (200 grams) granulated sugar
¼   cup (57 grams) unsalted butter, cubed and softened
½   cup (120 grams) heavy whipping cream, room temperature
½   teaspoon (2 grams) vanilla extract
¼   teaspoon kosher salt

1. In a medium heavy-bottomed saucepan, heat sugar over medium heat, stirring constantly with a heat-resistant spatula. Cook until sugar forms clumps and melts into a light amber-colored liquid, 4 to 5 minutes.
2. Once sugar is completely melted, carefully add butter, a few pieces at a time, whisking constantly until fully incorporated.
3. Slowly drizzle in cream, whisking constantly; boil for 1 minute. Remove from heat, and pour into a glass bowl or measuring cup. Stir in vanilla and salt. Let cool completely before using, about 2 hours. If caramel seems too runny once fully cooled, refrigerate for 15 to 30 minutes before filling cookies.

Note: *Salted Caramel Sauce can be made in advance and refrigerated for up to 2 weeks in an airtight container. Warm briefly before using.*

Photo by Laura Kasavan

STOLLEN MARZIPAN SHORTBREAD

Makes 24 cookies

Stollen, a classic German treat, packs booze-saturated fruit, ropes of marzipan, and warm, aromatic spices into a sweetened, yeasted bread loaf. This shortbread is a scaled-down affair, with rich, chewy Marzipan mixed directly into the dough and a buttery drizzle of Rum Glaze topping it off.

⅔   cup (150 grams) unsalted butter, softened
¼   cup (50 grams) granulated sugar
⅓   cup (100 grams) Marzipan (recipe follows)
1   large egg yolk (19 grams)
2   teaspoons (2 grams) orange zest
1   vanilla bean, split lengthwise, seeds scraped and reserved
2   cups (250 grams) all-purpose flour
¼   teaspoon kosher salt
⅛   teaspoon ground nutmeg
⅛   teaspoon ground ginger
Rum-Soaked Fruit (recipe follows)
Rum Glaze (recipe follows)

1. In the bowl of a stand mixer fitted with the paddle attachment, beat butter and sugar at medium speed until creamy, 3 to 4 minutes, stopping to scrape sides of bowl. Add Marzipan, and beat until well combined. Beat in egg yolk. Beat in zest and vanilla bean seeds.
2. In a medium bowl, sift together flour, salt, nutmeg, and ginger. With mixer on low speed, add flour mixture to butter mixture in two additions, letting first addition fully incorporate before adding the second. Stir in Rum-Soaked Fruit. Turn out dough, and shape into a 7-inch square. Wrap in plastic wrap, and refrigerate for 30 minutes.
3. Preheat oven to 325°F (170°C). Line a baking sheet with parchment paper.
4. Between 2 sheets of parchment paper, roll dough into a 9-inch square. Freeze for 15 minutes. Using a sharp knife, cut dough into 2¼x1½-inch rectangles. Place 1 inch apart on prepared pan. (If dough starts to soften, place back in freezer until firm again.)

5. Bake until lightly browned, 15 to 17 minutes. Let cool on pans for 3 minutes. Remove from pans, and let cool completely on wire racks. Pipe Rum Glaze over cooled cookies.

MARZIPAN
Makes about 1 cup

2¼   cups (216 grams) blanched almond flour
1½   cups (180 grams) confectioners' sugar
1   large egg white (30 grams)
2   teaspoons (8 grams) vanilla extract
2   teaspoons (8 grams) almond extract

1. In the work bowl of a food processor, place almond flour and confectioners' sugar; pulse until combined. Add egg white and extracts; process until mixture holds together. If mixture is too dry, add water, 1 teaspoon (5 grams) at a time. Wrap tightly in plastic wrap, and refrigerate for up to 1 month.

RUM-SOAKED FRUIT
Makes ¾ cup

¼   cup (32 grams) diced dried apricots
¼   cup (32 grams) dried cherries, halved
3   tablespoons (45 grams) dark spiced rum
2   tablespoons (24 grams) raisins
2   tablespoons (24 grams) golden raisins

1. In a small bowl, toss together all ingredients. Cover and let stand at room temperature overnight.

RUM GLAZE
Makes about ¾ cup

2   cups (240 grams) confectioners' sugar
3   tablespoons (45 grams) whole milk
2   tablespoons (30 grams) dark spiced rum

1. In a small bowl, stir together all ingredients until smooth. Use immediately.

APRICOT LINZER COOKIES

Makes 18 sandwich cookies

Almond flour makes for a nutty, slightly chewier shortbread, brightened by lemon zest in the dough. The Chambord raspberry liqueur in the filling has a sweet tang that plays up the tartness of the apricot. If you're anything like us, you'll splash what's left of the Loire Valley liqueur in a glass of bubbly to sip as you bake.

1 cup (227 grams) unsalted butter, softened
½ cup (100 grams) granulated sugar
2 cups (250 grams) all-purpose flour
½ cup (48 grams) blanched almond flour
1 teaspoon (1 gram) lemon zest
Apricot Raspberry Filling (recipe follows)
Garnish: confectioners' sugar

1. In the bowl of a stand mixer fitted with the paddle attachment, beat butter at low speed until smooth, 1 to 2 minutes. Add granulated sugar, beating until creamy, 2 to 3 minutes, stopping to scrape sides of bowl. Add flours and zest, beating until combined. Turn out dough, and shape into a disk. Wrap tightly in plastic wrap, and refrigerate for at least 2 hours or up to 5 days.

2. Preheat oven to 300°F (150°C). Line 3 baking sheets with parchment paper.

3. Let dough stand at room temperature until slightly softened, about 15 minutes. On a lightly floured surface, roll dough to ⅛-inch thickness. Using a 2½-inch fluted round cutter dipped in flour, cut dough, rerolling scraps and re-flouring cutter as necessary. Place on prepared pans. Using a 1-inch fluted round cutter, cut centers from half of cookies.

4. Bake until light golden brown around the edges, 20 to 25 minutes, rotating pans halfway through baking. Let cool on pans for 3 minutes. Remove from pans, and let cool completely on wire racks.

5. Spread 2 teaspoons Apricot Raspberry Filling on flat side of all solid cookies. Sprinkle cookies with cutouts with confectioners' sugar, if desired. Place cookies with cutouts, flat side down, on top of filling. Store in an airtight container at room temperature for up to 2 days.

APRICOT RASPBERRY FILLING

Makes 1 cup

1 cup (128 grams) chopped dried apricots
½ cup (120 grams) water
¼ cup (60 grams) raspberry liqueur*
2 tablespoons (24 grams) granulated sugar
1 teaspoon (4 grams) vanilla extract*

1. In a small saucepan, bring all ingredients to a boil over medium heat. Reduce heat to low; simmer for 10 minutes. Using an immersion blender, pulse until smooth. Refrigerate until ready to use.

We used Chambord Black Raspberry Liqueur and Heilala Vanilla Extract.

CANDIED CHERRY, DATE, AND PISTACHIO BISCOTTI

Makes 14 biscotti

With Candied Cherries and a little cherry brandy, this twice-baked Italian treat gets a double dose of cherry flavor. Chopped pistachios and sea salt flakes offset the sweet and lend the perfect amount of crunch. Dunk these in your coffee for the ultimate biscotti experience.

1   cup (200 grams) granulated sugar
½   cup (113 grams) unsalted butter, melted and cooled
3   tablespoons (45 grams) cherry brandy
1   teaspoon (4 grams) vanilla extract
Candied Cherries (recipe follows)
½   cup (64 grams) chopped dates
½   cup (57 grams) chopped pistachios
4   large eggs (200 grams), divided
2¾ cups (344 grams) all-purpose flour
1½ teaspoons (7.5 grams) baking powder
¼   teaspoon kosher salt
1   teaspoon (5 grams) water
2   tablespoons (24 grams) turbinado sugar
1   tablespoon (9 grams) sea salt

1. In a large bowl, stir together granulated sugar, melted butter, brandy, and vanilla. Add Candied Cherries, dates, pistachios, and 3 eggs (150 grams), stirring to combine.
2. In a medium bowl, whisk together flour, baking powder, and kosher salt. Gradually add flour mixture to sugar mixture, stirring just until combined. Cover and refrigerate for 30 minutes.
3. Preheat oven to 350°F (180°C).
4. On a lightly floured surface, shape dough into a 14x8-inch rectangle. Place on an ungreased baking sheet.
5. In a small bowl, whisk together 1 teaspoon (5 grams) water and remaining 1 egg (50 grams). Brush egg wash onto dough. Sprinkle with turbinado sugar and sea salt.
6. Bake until pale golden, about 30 minutes. Carefully transfer loaf to a wire rack to let cool for 15 minutes. Using a serrated knife, cut loaf into 1-inch slices. Return to baking sheet, cut side down. Bake until golden, about 15 minutes more, turning slices halfway through baking. Transfer to a wire rack to let cool completely. Store in an airtight container for up to 4 days.

CANDIED CHERRIES
Makes 1 cup

½   pound (227 grams) cherries, pitted and chopped
½   cup (100 grams) granulated sugar
½   cup (120 grams) fresh lemon juice
½   cup (120 grams) water

1. In a medium saucepan, combine all ingredients. Cook over medium heat, stirring frequently, until sugar is dissolved. Continue cooking until syrup is thick enough that it takes 2 seconds for liquid to close together when a spoon is passed through it, 30 to 35 minutes.
2. Preheat oven to 200°F (93°C). Line a baking sheet with parchment paper.
3. Transfer cherries to prepared pan, spreading to edges.
4. Bake until dry but tacky, 1½ to 2 hours. Refrigerate in an airtight container for up to 1 week.

BOURBON PECAN THUMBPRINT COOKIES

Makes 20 cookies

These nutty thumbprints are the classic Southern pairing of bourbon and pecans in cookie form. Chock-full of pecans, the cookie base gets smoky notes from bourbon, and a gooey bourbon, caramel, and toasted pecan filling rounds out every bite with sweetness.

⅓ cup (38 grams) chopped pecans
1⅓ cups (167 grams) all-purpose flour
¼ cup (32 grams) cornstarch
1 teaspoon (5 grams) baking powder
¾ teaspoon (2.25 grams) kosher salt
¼ cup plus 2 tablespoons (85 grams) unsalted butter, softened
¼ cup (50 grams) granulated sugar
¼ cup (55 grams) firmly packed light brown sugar
1 large egg (50 grams)
2 tablespoons (28 grams) canola oil
2 teaspoons (10 grams) bourbon
Bourbon Pecan Filling (recipe follows)
Garnish: pecan halves

1. Preheat oven to 350°F (180°C). Line 2 baking sheets with parchment paper.
2. In the work bowl of a food processor, pulse chopped pecans until finely ground. Transfer to a medium bowl; add flour, cornstarch, baking powder, and salt, whisking to combine. Set aside.
3. In the bowl of a stand mixer fitted with the paddle attachment, beat butter and sugars at medium speed until fluffy, 2 to 3 minutes, stopping to scrape sides of bowl. Add egg, oil, and bourbon, beating well. With mixer on low speed, gradually add pecan mixture to butter mixture, beating until combined.
4. Using a 1½-tablespoon spring-loaded scoop, scoop dough into mounds (about 30 grams each). Using floured hands, roll each mound into a smooth ball, and place 2 inches apart on prepared pans. Using your thumb or the handle of a wooden spoon, gently make an indentation in center of each ball that is deep enough to hold filling.
5. Bake until edges are lightly golden, 10 to 12 minutes. Remove from oven, and let cool on pans for 2 minutes. Remove from pans, and let cool completely on wire racks. Spoon about 1 teaspoon (6 grams) warm Bourbon Pecan Filling into center of each cookie. Top with pecan halves, if desired.

BOURBON PECAN FILLING
Makes about 1¼ cups

¾ cup (85 grams) chopped toasted pecans
½ cup (110 grams) firmly packed light brown sugar
⅓ cup (113 grams) dark corn syrup
2½ tablespoons (35 grams) unsalted butter
1 large egg (50 grams)
1 tablespoon (15 grams) bourbon
⅛ teaspoon kosher salt

1. In a medium saucepan, stir together all ingredients. Bring to a boil over medium-high heat, stirring frequently. Reduce heat to medium-low; simmer, stirring constantly, until thickened, 3 to 4 minutes. Use immediately.

Makes 15 sandwich cookies

Recipe by Edd Kimber

This play on the classic Oreo cookie hearkens back to a British classic, the mince pie. Originally made with meat, they're individual pies filled with a syrupy spiced fruit filling. These cookies follow the same pattern, served alongside a rum-infused buttercream.

¾   cup plus 2 tablespoons (198 grams) unsalted butter, softened
½   cup plus 2 tablespoons (124 grams) granulated sugar
½   cup plus 1 tablespoon (124 grams) firmly packed light brown sugar
1   teaspoon (4 grams) vanilla extract
2   cups plus 2 tablespoons (266 grams) all-purpose flour
½   cup (43 grams) black cocoa powder
½   teaspoon (2.5 grams) baking soda
½   teaspoon (1.5 grams) kosher salt
Rum Buttercream (recipe follows)
Quick Mincemeat Filling (recipe follows)
Garnish: confectioners' sugar

1. In the bowl of a stand mixer fitted with the paddle attachment, beat butter, granulated sugar, and brown sugar at medium speed until fluffy, 2 to 3 minutes, stopping to scrape sides of bowl. Beat in vanilla.
2. In a medium bowl, whisk together flour, black cocoa, baking soda, and salt. With mixer on low speed, gradually add flour mixture to butter mixture, beating just until dough starts to come together. (If you overmix the dough, your cookies will end up chewy rather than crisp.) Turn out dough onto a work surface, and bring together into a uniform dough. Divide dough in half, and shape each half into a disk. Wrap in plastic wrap, and refrigerate for at least 1 hour.
3. Preheat oven to 350°F (180°C). Line 2 half sheet pans with parchment paper.
4. On a lightly floured surface, roll half of dough to ⅛-inch thickness. Using a 2¾-inch fluted round cutter, cut dough, reserving scraps. Place cookies on prepared pans. Using a 1-inch star-shaped cutter, cut centers from half of cookies. Repeat with remaining dough. Gather all scraps, and briefly knead back into a uniform dough. Refrigerate until firm before repeating procedure once. (Don't use the second round of scraps because working the dough further will make tough cookies.) Refrigerate cookies for 20 minutes.
5. Bake until firm, about 9 minutes. Let cool on pans for 10 minutes. Remove from pans, and let cool completely on wire racks.
6. Place Rum Buttercream in a piping bag fitted with a small round piping tip. Pipe a ring of Rum Buttercream on flat side of all solid cookies. Fill centers with Quick Mincemeat Filling. Dust cookies with cutouts with confectioners' sugar, if desired. Place cookies with cutouts, flat side down, on top of filling. Store in an airtight container for up to 3 days.

MINCEMEAT RUM CHOCOLATE SANDWICH COOKIES

RUM BUTTERCREAM
Makes 1½ cups

½   cup (113 grams) unsalted butter, softened
2   cups (240 grams) confectioners' sugar
2   tablespoons (30 grams) spiced rum
1   teaspoon (4 grams) vanilla extract
⅛   teaspoon kosher salt

1. In the bowl of a stand mixer fitted with the paddle attachment, beat butter at medium speed until smooth and creamy. Add confectioners' sugar, and beat until fluffy, about 5 minutes. Add rum, vanilla, and salt, and beat until combined, about 1 minute. Use immediately.

QUICK MINCEMEAT FILLING
Makes 1 cup

1   orange (131 grams), zested and juiced
½   cup (64 grams) sultanas
½   cup (64 grams) raisins
¼   cup (55 grams) firmly packed light brown sugar
1   teaspoon (2 grams) mixed spice*
2   tablespoons (30 grams) spiced rum

1. In a small saucepan, combine orange zest and juice, sultanas, raisins, brown sugar, and mixed spice. Cook over medium-high heat until sugar is dissolved and liquid has reduced and become syrupy. Remove from heat; stir in rum. Cover with plastic wrap, and refrigerate until ready to use. When fully cooled, mixture should be thick like caramel. If too loose, it needs to cook slightly longer.

Mixed spice, available at amazon.com, is the most traditional British spice mix used in most classic Christmas fruit dessert recipes. You can substitute with pumpkin pie spice, available at American grocery stores, or make your own mixed spice. Stir together 1 tablespoon (6 grams) ground allspice, 1 tablespoon (6 grams) ground cinnamon, 1 tablespoon (6 grams) ground nutmeg, 2 teaspoons (4 grams) ground ginger, ½ teaspoon (1 gram) ground cloves, and ½ teaspoon (1 gram) ground coriander.

Photo by Edd Kimber

[boozy]

CHOCOLATE-BOURBON PEANUT BUTTER COOKIES

Makes about 40 cookies

Your favorite Girl Scout cookie is all grown up. A dose of bourbon in the crumbly sablé dough and peanut butter filling give this cookie a subtle kick you can't find in the boxed version from your local troop.

¾   cup plus 2 tablespoons (198 grams) unsalted butter, softened
⅓   cup (40 grams) confectioners' sugar
¼   cup (50 grams) granulated sugar
1   teaspoon (3 grams) kosher salt
1   large egg yolk (19 grams)
1   teaspoon (5 grams) bourbon
1   teaspoon (6 grams) vanilla bean paste
2   cups (250 grams) all-purpose flour
⅓   cup plus 1 tablespoon (38 grams) blanched almond meal
Bourbon Peanut Butter (recipe follows)
1   (10-ounce) bag (283.8 grams) 60% cacao dark chocolate melting wafers

1. In the bowl of a stand mixer fitted with the paddle attachment, beat butter at medium-low speed until smooth, about 1 minute. Add sugars and salt, and beat until smooth, about 1 minute. Add egg yolk, bourbon, and vanilla bean paste, and beat until combined, about 1 minute.

2. In a medium bowl, whisk together flour and almond meal. With mixer on low speed, add flour mixture to butter mixture in two additions, beating just until combined. Turn out dough onto a lightly floured surface, and gently knead 3 to 4 times. Between 2 large sheets of parchment paper, roll dough to ¼-inch thickness. Transfer dough between parchment to refrigerator. Refrigerate until set, at least 2 hours.

3. Preheat oven to 325°F (170°C). Line 2 baking sheets with parchment paper.

4. Using a 1¾-inch round cutter dipped in flour, cut dough, and place at least ½ inch apart on prepared pans. Reroll scraps between parchment, and freeze until set, about 5 minutes, if necessary, before cutting dough.

5. Bake, one batch at a time, until bottom edges of cookies turn golden, 12 to 14 minutes. Let cool on pans for 5 minutes. Remove from pans, and let cool completely on wire racks.

6. Place Bourbon Peanut Butter in a disposable piping bag, and cut a ½-inch-wide hole in tip. Pipe Bourbon Peanut Butter in a spiral pattern on top of each cookie. Place a small sheet of wax paper over each cookie, and smooth Bourbon Peanut Butter flat and even with edges of cookie. Remove wax paper. Refrigerate until set, about 20 minutes.

7. In a large microwave-safe bowl, heat chocolate on medium for 30 seconds, and stir; microwave in 15-second intervals, stirring between each, until melted and smooth. Let cool slightly, 3 to 5 minutes. Place each cookie in melted chocolate; using a fork, lift cookies out of chocolate, and gently tap on side of bowl to remove excess. Place cookies on a sheet pan lined with parchment paper. Refrigerate until chocolate is set, 5 to 10 minutes.

BOURBON PEANUT BUTTER
Makes about 2 cups

1   cup (256 grams) creamy peanut butter
6   tablespoons (90 grams) heavy whipping cream
1   cup (120 grams) confectioners' sugar
2   tablespoons (30 grams) bourbon

1. In a medium bowl, beat peanut butter and cream with a mixer at medium speed until smooth. Gradually add confectioners' sugar, beating until combined. Beat in bourbon. Use immediately.

IRISH CREAM THUMBPRINT COOKIES

Makes 18 cookies

Calling all coffeeholics: this one's for you. An Irish Cream Filling rests on a buttery, espresso-packed cookie for a thumbprint that's sure to deliver that much-needed caffeine kick.

¼ cup plus 2 tablespoons (85 grams) unsalted butter, softened
½ cup (110 grams) firmly packed dark brown sugar
1   large egg (50 grams)
2   tablespoons (28 grams) canola oil
2   teaspoons (12 grams) vanilla bean paste
1½ cups (188 grams) all-purpose flour
3   tablespoons (24 grams) cornstarch
1   tablespoon (6 grams) espresso powder
1   teaspoon (5 grams) baking powder
½ teaspoon (1.5 grams) kosher salt
Irish Cream Filling (recipe follows)
Garnish: espresso powder

1. Preheat oven to 350°F (180°C). Line 2 baking sheets with parchment paper.
2. In the bowl of a stand mixer fitted with the paddle attachment, beat butter and brown sugar at medium speed until fluffy, 2 to 3 minutes, stopping to scrape sides of bowl. Add egg, oil, and vanilla bean paste, beating well.
3. In a medium bowl, whisk together flour, cornstarch, espresso powder, baking powder, and salt. With mixer on low speed, gradually add flour mixture to butter mixture, beating until combined.
4. Using a 1½-tablespoon spring-loaded scoop, scoop dough (about 30 grams each), and place 2 inches apart on prepared pans. Using your thumb or the handle of a wooden spoon, gently make an indentation in center of each ball.
5. Bake until edges are lightly golden, 8 to 10 minutes. Let cool on pans for 2 minutes. Remove from pans, and let cool completely on wire racks. Spoon about 1 teaspoon (6 grams) Irish Cream Filling into center of each cookie. Let set before serving. Garnish with espresso powder, if desired.

IRISH CREAM FILLING
Makes about ½ cup

1   cup (120 grams) confectioners' sugar
2   tablespoons plus 1 teaspoon (35 grams) Irish cream liqueur*

1. In a small bowl, whisk together confectioners' sugar and liqueur until smooth. Use immediately.

We used Baileys Original Irish Cream.

STOP, DROP, AND BAKE

WHEN WEEKNIGHT CRAVINGS CALL, THESE DROP COOKIES COME TOGETHER IN A FLASH. FROM INDULGENT CRINKLE COOKIES TO CHEWY PISTACHIO MACAROONS, THESE RECIPES DELIVER SATISFACTION ON DEMAND.

CHOCOLATE PEPPERMINT COOKIES

Makes about 45 cookies

These addictive cookies get a creamy boost from milk chocolate chips and a hint of crisp mint from peppermint extract. Crushed candy canes speckle the top for a traditional wintry finish.

1½ cups (340 grams) unsalted butter, softened
1¼ cups (275 grams) firmly packed light brown sugar
½ cup (100 grams) granulated sugar
3 large eggs (150 grams)
2 teaspoons (8 grams) vanilla extract
½ teaspoon (2 grams) peppermint extract
3¼ cups (406 grams) all-purpose flour
1 cup (85 grams) Dutch process cocoa powder
1½ teaspoons (4.5 grams) kosher salt
1 teaspoon (5 grams) baking soda
2½ cups (425 grams) milk chocolate chips
½ cup (75 grams) candy cane pieces

1. In the bowl of a stand mixer fitted with the paddle attachment, beat butter and sugars at medium speed until fluffy, 2 to 3 minutes, stopping to scrape sides of bowl. Reduce mixer speed to medium-low. Add eggs, one at a time, beating well after each addition. Beat in extracts.
2. In a large bowl, whisk together flour, cocoa, salt, and baking soda. With mixer on low speed, gradually add flour mixture to butter mixture, beating just until combined. (Do not overmix.) Gently stir in chocolate chips. Refrigerate for 30 minutes.
3. Preheat oven to 350°F (180°C). Line rimmed baking sheets with parchment paper.
4. Using a 2-tablespoon spring-loaded scoop, scoop dough, and drop at least 2 inches apart onto prepared pans.
5. Bake, one batch at a time, for 16 minutes, rotating pans halfway through baking. Remove from oven, and immediately sprinkle ½ teaspoon candy cane pieces on top of each cookie. Let cool on pans for 5 minutes. Using a thin spatula, remove from pans, and let cool completely on wire racks. Store in an airtight container at room temperature for up to 5 days.

OATMEAL CHERRY WALNUT COOKIES

Makes about 24 cookies

Recipe by Marian Cooper Cairns

Who needs raisins when you can have a much bigger, even sweeter flavor impact with plump dried cherries? If walnuts are not your jam, pecans or hazelnuts are great substitutes. Be sure to toast the nuts for optimal flavor. Baking at 350°F (180°C) until the nuts smell slightly fragrant, about 8 minutes, will do the trick.

1	cup (227 grams) unsalted butter, softened
1	cup (220 grams) firmly packed dark brown sugar
1	cup (200 grams) granulated sugar
2	large eggs (100 grams)
2	teaspoons (8 grams) vanilla extract
2	cups (250 grams) all-purpose flour
1	teaspoon (5 grams) baking powder
1	teaspoon (5 grams) baking soda
1	teaspoon (3 grams) kosher salt
¾	teaspoon (1.5 grams) ground cinnamon
½	teaspoon (1 gram) ground nutmeg
3	cups (240 grams) old-fashioned oats
1½	cups (192 grams) coarsely chopped dried cherries
1½	cups (170 grams) coarsely chopped toasted walnuts

1. Preheat oven to 350°F (180°C). Line 2 baking sheets with parchment paper.
2. In the bowl of a stand mixer fitted with the paddle attachment, beat butter and sugars at medium speed until fluffy, about 2 minutes, stopping to scrape sides of bowl. Add eggs and vanilla, beating until combined.
3. In a medium bowl, whisk together flour, baking powder, baking soda, salt, cinnamon, and nutmeg. With mixer on low speed, gradually add flour mixture to butter mixture, beating just until combined. Beat in oats, cherries, and walnuts. Working in 2 batches, drop dough by 3 tablespoonfuls 2 inches apart onto prepared pans. (For picture-perfect cookies, press a few walnuts and cherries onto exterior of each dough ball.)
4. Bake until golden but still slightly soft in center, 15 to 18 minutes, rotating pans once. Let cool on pans for 3 minutes. Remove from pans, and let cool completely on wire racks.

Photo by Matt Armendariz

EGGNOG DROP COOKIES

Makes about 30 cookies

Your favorite holiday toddy gets the cookie send-up it deserves. Nutmeg, cloves, cinnamon, and spiced rum come together in these simple, tender drop cookies for a perfectly balanced eggnog flavor.

¾   cup (170 grams) unsalted butter, softened
¾   cup (165 grams) firmly packed light brown sugar
¼   cup (50 grams) granulated sugar
2   large egg yolks (37 grams)
1   teaspoon (4 grams) vanilla extract
½   teaspoon (2 grams) rum extract
½   teaspoon (2 grams) maple syrup extract
2¼   cups (281 grams) all-purpose flour
2   teaspoons (10 grams) baking powder
1   teaspoon (2 grams) ground nutmeg
½   teaspoon (1.5 grams) kosher salt
½   teaspoon (1 gram) ground cinnamon
¼   teaspoon ground cloves
¼   cup (60 grams) spiced rum
¼   cup (60 grams) heavy whipping cream
Vanilla Buttercream (recipe follows)
Garnish: grated fresh nutmeg

1. Preheat oven to 350°F (180°C). Line 3 baking sheets with parchment paper.
2. In the bowl of a stand mixer fitted with the paddle attachment, beat butter and sugars at medium speed until fluffy, 3 to 4 minutes, stopping to scrape sides of bowl. Add egg yolks, one at a time, beating just until combined after each addition. Beat in extracts.
3. In a medium bowl, whisk together flour, baking powder, nutmeg, salt, cinnamon, and cloves. In a small bowl, combine rum and cream. With mixer on low speed, gradually add flour mixture to butter mixture alternately with rum mixture, beginning and ending with flour mixture, beating just until combined after each addition. Using a 1½-tablespoon spring-loaded scoop, scoop dough, and drop 2 inches apart onto prepared pans. Press down to flatten slightly.

4. Bake until lightly golden, 10 to 12 minutes. Let cool on pans for 5 minutes. Remove from pans, and let cool completely on wire racks. Spread Vanilla Buttercream onto cooled cookies. Garnish with nutmeg, if desired. Store in an airtight container at room temperature for up to 4 days.

Vanilla Buttercream

Makes about 3 cups

½   cup (113 grams) unsalted butter, softened
3   cups (360 grams) confectioners' sugar
2   tablespoons (30 grams) heavy whipping cream
1   teaspoon (4 grams) vanilla extract

1. In the bowl of a stand mixer fitted with the paddle attachment, beat all ingredients at medium-low speed until light and fluffy, 2 to 3 minutes. Use immediately.

FLOURLESS FUDGY COOKIES

Makes 16 cookies

A cross between a dense brownie and a chewy cookie, these flourless cocoa-rich cookies are a tour de force in texture and taste.

3 large egg whites (90 grams), room temperature
2 teaspoons (12 grams) vanilla bean paste
2 cups plus 2 tablespoons (255 grams) confectioners' sugar
1 cup (85 grams) Dutch process cocoa powder
¼ teaspoon kosher salt
1 cup (170 grams) 63% cacao dark chocolate chips
16 walnut halves
Garnish: finishing salt

1. Line 2 baking sheets with parchment paper, and spray with cooking spray.
2. In a large bowl, whisk together egg whites and vanilla bean paste. Add confectioners' sugar, cocoa, and kosher salt, whisking until smooth. Fold in chocolate chips.
3. Using a 1½-tablespoon spring-loaded scoop, scoop dough (about 30 grams each), and drop onto prepared pans. Place a walnut half in center of each cookie. Let stand at room temperature for 30 minutes.
4. Preheat oven to 350°F (180°C).
5. Bake for 10 minutes. Let cool completely on pans. Top with finishing salt, if desired.

LEMON SUGAR COOKIES

Makes about 38 cookies

Like a burst of bright, edible sunshine, these Lemon Sugar Cookies come complete with crunchy sanding sugar and a zest-packed Lemon Glaze.

1   cup (227 grams) unsalted butter, softened
½   cup (112 grams) cream cheese, softened
1   cup (200 grams) granulated sugar
½   cup (110 grams) firmly packed light brown sugar
2   large eggs (100 grams), room temperature
1½   tablespoons (4.5 grams) lemon zest
1   teaspoon (4 grams) vanilla extract
3½   cups (438 grams) all-purpose flour
1   teaspoon (5 grams) baking powder
¼   teaspoon (1.25 grams) baking soda
¼   teaspoon kosher salt
Sanding sugar, for sprinkling
Lemon Glaze (recipe follows)

1. In the bowl of a stand mixer fitted with the paddle attachment, beat butter and cream cheese at medium-high speed until smooth, 2 to 3 minutes. Reduce mixer speed to low. Add granulated sugar and brown sugar, beating until combined. Increase mixer speed to medium-high, and beat until fluffy, 2 to 3 minutes, stopping to scrape sides of bowl. Add eggs, zest, and vanilla, beating to combine.
2. In a medium bowl, whisk together flour, baking powder, baking soda, and salt. With mixer on low speed, gradually add flour mixture to butter mixture, beating until combined. Increase mixer speed to medium; beat 1 to 2 minutes more. Cover with plastic wrap, and refrigerate for 1 hour.

3. Preheat oven to 350°F (180°C). Line baking sheets with parchment paper.
4. Using a 1½-tablespoon spring-loaded scoop, scoop dough (about 30 grams each), and drop 2 inches apart onto prepared pans. Sprinkle with sanding sugar.
5. Bake until edges are lightly browned, 8 to 10 minutes. Let cool on pans for 5 minutes. Remove from pans, and let cool completely on wire racks. Spoon Lemon Glaze over cooled cookies. Sprinkle with sanding sugar.

LEMON GLAZE
Makes about ¾ cup

2   cups (240 grams) confectioners' sugar
2   lemons (198 grams), zested and juiced

1. In a small bowl, whisk together confectioners' sugar and lemon zest and juice until smooth. Use immediately.

EARL GREY CHOCOLATE CRINKLE COOKIES

Makes about 40 cookies

It's time to upgrade your crinkle cookie game! The citrusy, floral flavor of Earl Grey tea adds an elegant note to these dramatic, ultradecadent chocolate treats.

1	cup (125 grams) all-purpose flour
½	cup (43 grams) unsweetened Dutch process cocoa powder*
2	tablespoons (12 grams) finely ground Earl Grey tea (about 7 tea bags)
1¾	teaspoons (8.75 grams) baking powder
¾	teaspoon (2.25 grams) kosher salt
1¼	cups (250 grams) plus ⅓ cup (67 grams) granulated sugar, divided
3	large eggs (150 grams), room temperature
4	ounces (115 grams) unsweetened baking chocolate*, chopped
¼	cup (57 grams) unsalted butter
⅓	cup (40 grams) confectioners' sugar, sifted

1. Preheat oven to 325°F (170°C). Line 2 rimmed baking sheets with parchment paper.

2. In a medium bowl, whisk together flour, cocoa, tea, baking powder, and salt. In a large bowl, combine 1¼ cups (250 grams) granulated sugar and eggs. Set aside.

3. In a medium microwave-safe bowl, combine chopped chocolate and butter. Microwave on high in 10-second intervals, stirring between each, until melted and smooth. Slowly whisk chocolate mixture into egg mixture; fold in flour mixture until well combined and no dry streaks remain. Let dough stand at room temperature for 20 minutes.

4. Place confectioners' sugar and remaining ⅓ cup (67 grams) granulated sugar in separate small bowls. Working with one at a time, shape dough into 1-tablespoon balls. Drop in granulated sugar, coating completely. Roll in confectioners' sugar, and place 1 to 1½ inches apart on prepared pans.

5. Bake until edges are just set and cracks have formed, about 10 minutes. Let cool completely on pans.

*We used Valrhona 100% Cacao Cocoa Powder and Guittard Unsweetened Chocolate Gourmet Baking Bars.

MAKE AHEAD TIP
Measure out and combine flour, cocoa, tea, baking powder, and salt. Cover with plastic wrap, and store at room temperature until ready to use.

PISTACHIO AND COCONUT MACAROONS

Makes about 27 cookies

Packed with toasted coconut and dipped in chocolate, it's no wonder the macaroon is a classic. We twirled it up by adding ground pistachios to the coconut mix, playing up the cookie's signature sweetness with earthy, nutty notes.

1   (14-ounce) package (396 grams) sweetened
     shredded coconut*
⅔   cup (64 grams) ground roasted salted pistachios
½   cup (63 grams) pastry flour
½   cup (57 grams) chopped roasted salted pistachios
1   cup (200 grams) granulated sugar
½   cup (120 grams) egg whites
Garnish: melted dark chocolate

1. Preheat oven to 350°F (180°C). Line baking sheets with parchment paper.
2. In a medium bowl, whisk together coconut, ground pistachios, flour, and chopped pistachios. Set aside.
3. In the top of a double boiler, stir together sugar and egg whites. Cook over simmering water until mixture registers 120°F (49°C) on an instant-read thermometer. Remove from heat; stir in coconut mixture. Return to heat, and heat until mixture registers 110°F (43°C). Remove from heat; cover and let stand for 5 minutes.
4. Using a 1½-tablespoon spring-loaded scoop, scoop mixture (about 33 grams each), and drop at least 1 inch apart onto prepared pans. To keep exteriors of macaroons smooth, use your fingertips to gently press in coconut bits.
5. Bake until bottoms are golden, about 15 minutes. Let cool completely on pans. Dip bottom of each cookie in melted chocolate, if desired. Refrigerate until chocolate is set, 5 to 10 minutes.

We used Baker's Angel Flake Shredded Coconut.

CAFÉ MOCHA COOKIES

Makes 24 cookies

Our mocha brownie cookies positively crackle with ground chocolate-covered coffee beans and freshly brewed espresso in the dough, but for the ultimate finish, we opted for a generous swoop of dulce de leche.

1½   cups (255 grams) 63% cacao dark chocolate chips
¼   cup (57 grams) unsalted butter, softened
1¼   cups (192 grams) dark chocolate-covered coffee beans
3   large eggs (150 grams), room temperature
1   cup (200 grams) granulated sugar
¾   cup (94 grams) all-purpose flour
¾   teaspoon (3.75 grams) baking powder
¾   teaspoon (2.25 grams) kosher salt
2   tablespoons (30 grams) brewed espresso, cooled
1½   teaspoons (6 grams) vanilla extract
1   cup (304 grams) dulce de leche*
Garnish: flaked sea salt, crushed coffee beans

1. In the top of a double boiler, combine chocolate chips and butter. Cook over simmering water, stirring frequently, until melted and smooth. Let cool to room temperature.
2. Preheat oven to 350°F (180°C). Line baking sheets with parchment paper.
3. In the work bowl of a food processor, pulse chocolate-covered coffee beans until most of beans are finely ground; set aside.
4. In the bowl of a stand mixer fitted with the whisk attachment, beat eggs and sugar at high speed until very thick and pale, 5 to 6 minutes. With mixer on low speed, add cooled chocolate mixture in three additions, beating until combined after each addition.

5. In a medium bowl, whisk together flour, baking powder, and kosher salt. With mixer on low speed, gradually add flour mixture to egg mixture, beating just until combined, stopping to scrape sides of bowl. Beat in cooled espresso and vanilla. Fold in ground chocolate-covered coffee beans.
6. Drop batter by 2 tablespoonfuls (35 to 40 grams) about 2 inches apart onto prepared pans. (Batter will be very loose, similar to brownie batter. Use a small spatula to cleanly drop batter from tablespoon scoop.)
7. Bake until puffed and cracked, 12 to 13 minutes. Let cool completely on pans. Store in airtight containers between layers of parchment paper at room temperature until ready to serve.
8. To serve, spread dulce de leche onto cookies. Sprinkle with sea salt and crushed coffee beans, if desired.

We used Nestlé La Lechera Dulce de Leche.

COOKIES & CREAM COOKIES

Makes about 30 cookies

Like your favorite cookie and beverage combo, only turned inside out and made twice as delicious. Vanilla-scented white chocolate studs this chewy black cocoa cookie.

¾   cup (170 grams) unsalted butter, softened
¾   cup (150 grams) granulated sugar
¾   cup (165 grams) firmly packed dark brown sugar
1   large egg (50 grams)
1   large egg yolk (19 grams)
2   teaspoons (12 grams) vanilla bean paste
1¼   cups (156 grams) all-purpose flour
¾   cup (64 grams) black cocoa powder
1   teaspoon (5 grams) baking powder
1   teaspoon (3 grams) kosher salt
¼   teaspoon (1.25 gram) baking soda
2½   cups (425 grams) chopped white chocolate*

1. Line a rimmed baking sheet with parchment paper.
2. In the bowl of a stand mixer fitted with the paddle attachment, beat butter and sugars at medium speed until fluffy, 2 to 3 minutes, stopping to scrape sides of bowl. Add egg and egg yolk, one at a time, beating well after each addition. Beat in vanilla bean paste.
3. In a medium bowl, whisk together flour, black cocoa, baking powder, salt, and baking soda. With mixer on low speed, gradually add flour mixture to butter mixture, beating just until combined. Stir in chopped chocolate. Using a 1.5-ounce spring-loaded scoop, scoop dough (about 40 grams each), and place on prepared pan. Cover and refrigerate for at least 2 hours or overnight.
4. Preheat oven to 350°F (180°C). Line 4 baking sheets with parchment paper.
5. Place chilled dough at least 2½ inches apart on prepared pans.
6. For a soft center, bake for 10 to 12 minutes. For a crispy cookie, bake for 14 minutes. Rotate pans halfway through baking. Let cool on pans for 5 minutes. Remove from pans, and let cool completely on wire racks. Serve warm or at room temperature.

*Because they have hints of vanilla, we like to use Valhrona Ivoire 35% Baking Bars or Guittard Choc au Lait Baking Chips.

SPICE
IT UP

THESE COOKIES PACK A LITTLE EXTRA KICK FROM CINNAMON, GINGER, AND EVERY SPICE IN BETWEEN. TRY CHOCOLATE-DIPPED BISCOTTI, VANILLA CHAI PINWHEEL COOKIES, CARDAMOM-SCENTED PALMIERS, AND MORE.

MOLASSES, GINGER, AND CARDAMOM SPICE COOKIES

Makes 18 cookies

Recipe by Edd Kimber

Toasty and gently spiced with a unique molasses flavor, these cookies epitomize all a holiday cookie should be. With the addition of fresh ginger and a heavy dose of cardamom, they have a little more depth than the traditional spice cookie.

1	cup (227 grams) unsalted butter, softened
1⅓	cups (293 grams) firmly packed light brown sugar
¼	cup (85 grams) molasses
2	tablespoons (35 grams) grated fresh ginger
1	large egg (50 grams)
1	teaspoon (4 grams) vanilla extract
3¼	cups (406 grams) all-purpose flour
2	teaspoons (10 grams) baking soda
2	teaspoons (4 grams) freshly ground cardamom
1	teaspoon (2 grams) ground ginger
½	teaspoon (1.5 grams) kosher salt
½	teaspoon (1 gram) ground cinnamon
½	cup (100 grams) granulated sugar

1. Preheat oven to 350°F (180°C). Line 2 half sheet pans with parchment paper.
2. In the bowl of a stand mixer fitted with the paddle attachment, beat butter, brown sugar, molasses, and grated ginger at medium speed until fluffy, 2 to 3 minutes, stopping to scrape sides of bowl. Add egg and vanilla, beating until combined.
3. In a medium bowl, whisk together flour, baking soda, cardamom, ground ginger, salt, and cinnamon. With mixer on low speed, gradually add flour mixture to butter mixture, beating just until combined. Cover bowl with plastic wrap, and refrigerate for 1 hour. (Baking straight away will make the cookies spread a little too much.)
4. Using a ¼-cup scoop, scoop dough, and roll into balls. Roll balls in granulated sugar, coating completely. Place 2 inches apart on prepared pans.
5. Bake until slightly puffed and cracked all over, 13 to 14 minutes. Remove from oven, and tap pan sharply on a work surface to slightly collapse cookies. (This will give the center of the cookies a soft texture and the outside a slight chew.) Let cool on pans for 5 minutes. Remove from pans, and let cool completely on wire racks. Store in an airtight container for up to 5 days.

Photo by Edd Kimber

SPICED CHINESE ALMOND COOKIES

Makes 30 cookies

Recipe by Rebecca Firth

This is your new favorite holiday cookie that you didn't know you needed. The classic, crisp Chinese takeout almond cookie takes on an updated, soft-batch vibe in these super spiced-up renditions. Be sure to add a thorough coat of the egg wash—it'll give it that über nostalgic, lacquered appearance.

1	cup (227 grams) unsalted butter, softened
1¼	cups (250 grams) granulated sugar
1	large egg (50 grams), room temperature
1	teaspoon (4 grams) almond extract
1¾	cups (219 grams) all-purpose flour
¾	cup (95 grams) bread flour
½	cup (48 grams) blanched almond flour
1	teaspoon (5 grams) baking powder
1	teaspoon (5 grams) baking soda
1	teaspoon (2 grams) ground cinnamon
½	teaspoon (1.5 grams) sea salt
½	teaspoon (1 gram) ground allspice
½	teaspoon (1 gram) ground nutmeg
30	whole raw almonds (34 grams)
1	large egg yolk (19 grams)
2	tablespoons (30 grams) heavy whipping cream

1. Preheat oven to 350°F (180°C). Line several baking sheets with parchment paper.

2. In the bowl of a stand mixer fitted with the paddle attachment, beat butter and sugar at medium speed until fluffy, 2 to 3 minutes, stopping to scrape sides of bowl. Add egg and almond extract, and beat until well combined, about 2 minutes.

3. In a medium bowl, whisk together flours, baking powder, baking soda, cinnamon, sea salt, allspice, and nutmeg. With mixer on low speed, gradually add flour mixture to butter mixture, beating just until combined. Using a spatula, scrape sides and bottom of bowl to ensure everything is incorporated.

4. Using a 1½-tablespoon scoop, scoop dough, and roll into balls. Place 2 inches apart on prepared pans. Press an almond into center of each ball, and gently flatten into a disk.

5. In a small bowl, whisk together egg yolk and cream. Brush egg wash onto top and sides of dough, making sure it is thoroughly covered in wash but not pooling around base of dough.

6. Bake until bronzed, 12 to 13 minutes. Hold pans several inches above counter, and drop to deflate cookies slightly. Let cool on pans for 5 to 10 minutes. Remove from pans, and let cool completely on wire racks.

Photo by Rebecca Firth

ROASTED BLOOD ORANGE HAZELNUT BISCOTTI

Makes about 48 biscotti

Recipe by Marian Cooper Cairns

These biscotti take the classic pairing of chocolate and citrus to the next level. Sliced-up fresh blood oranges are tossed in honey and roasted to golden perfection. Roasting the oranges gives the biscotti an even deeper citrus flavor.

2	blood oranges (262 grams), peeled
3	tablespoons (63 grams) honey
6	tablespoons (84 grams) unsalted butter, softened
¾	cup (150 grams) granulated sugar
2	large eggs (100 grams)
1	tablespoon (3 grams) blood orange zest
2	teaspoons (8 grams) vanilla extract
2¼	cups (281 grams) all-purpose flour
1½	teaspoons (7.5 grams) baking powder
1	teaspoon (3 grams) kosher salt
½	teaspoon (1 gram) ground cinnamon
¾	cup (106 grams) toasted hazelnuts, chopped
8	ounces (225 grams) dark chocolate, chopped

Garnish: roasted sliced blood oranges

1. Preheat oven to 400°F (200°C). Line a baking sheet with parchment paper.
2. Cut blood oranges into ⅛-inch-thick slices, discarding seeds. In a medium bowl, toss together oranges and honey. Arrange in a single layer on prepared pan.
3. Bake until edges are just beginning to brown, 20 to 25 minutes, rotating pan once. Let cool completely on wire racks. (Set aside a few slices for garnish, if desired.) Chop into ½-inch pieces.
4. Reduce oven temperature to 325°F (170°C). Line a large baking sheet with parchment paper.
5. In the bowl of a stand mixer fitted with the paddle attachment, beat butter and sugar at medium speed until fluffy, about 2 minutes, stopping to scrape sides of bowl. Add eggs, one at a time, beating well after each addition. Beat in zest and vanilla.
6. In a medium bowl, whisk together flour, baking powder, salt, and cinnamon. With mixer on low speed, gradually add flour mixture to butter mixture, beating until combined. Stir in chopped roasted oranges and hazelnuts. Using lightly floured hands, divide dough in half. Shape each half into a 12x4-inch log. Place logs on prepared pan.
7. Bake until firm to the touch, about 28 minutes. Let cool on pan for 15 minutes. Using a serrated knife, cut logs into ½-inch-thick, slightly diagonal slices. Place slices, cut side down, on baking sheet.
8. Bake for 9 minutes. Turn biscotti over, and bake until dry, about 12 minutes more. Let cool completely on wire racks.
9. In a small microwave-safe bowl, microwave three-fourths of chocolate on medium in 30-second intervals, stirring between each, until melted and smooth. Stir in remaining one-fourth of chocolate until melted. Dip one end of each biscotti in melted chocolate. Place on a lightly greased wire rack, and let stand until set, about 1 hour. Garnish with roasted orange slices, if desired.

Photo by Matt Armendariz

SPICED CRANBERRY BARK COOKIES

Makes 36 cookies

Recipe by Rebecca Firth

Picture the very yummiest chocolate chip cookie, but then swap out the usual chocolate chips for a homemade chocolate bark that's loaded with toasted hazelnuts, fresh cranberries, spices, and sea salt flakes. This would be a great recipe to experiment with and swap in some other favorite fruit and nut combinations.

10 tablespoons (140 grams) unsalted butter, softened
1¼ cups (275 grams) firmly packed light brown sugar
½ cup (100 grams) granulated sugar
⅓ cup (75 grams) sunflower seed oil or other neutral oil
2 large eggs (100 grams), room temperature
2 tablespoons (30 grams) milk, room temperature
1 tablespoon (13 grams) vanilla extract
2 cups (260 grams) all-purpose flour
1 cup (127 grams) bread flour
2 teaspoons (10 grams) baking powder
1 teaspoon (5 grams) baking soda
1 teaspoon (3 grams) sea salt
1 teaspoon (2 grams) ground cinnamon
½ teaspoon (1 gram) ground nutmeg
Cranberry Bark (recipe follows), coarsely chopped
Flaked sea salt, for sprinkling

1. Preheat oven to 350°F (180°C). Line several baking sheets with parchment paper.
2. In the bowl of a stand mixer fitted with the paddle attachment, beat butter, sugars, and oil at medium speed until fluffy, 2 to 3 minutes, stopping to scrape sides of bowl. Add eggs, one at a time, beating well after each addition. With mixer on low speed, add milk and vanilla, beating until well combined, about 1 minute.

3. In a medium bowl, whisk together flours, baking powder, baking soda, sea salt, cinnamon, and nutmeg. Gradually add flour mixture to butter mixture, beating just until combined. (You still want some streaks of flour.) Fold Cranberry Bark into dough until evenly distributed. Let dough stand at room temperature for 15 minutes.
4. Scoop dough by 2 tablespoonfuls, and roll into balls. Place about 2 inches apart on prepared pans.
5. Bake for 11 to 12 minutes. Tap pans on counter once, and sprinkle with flaked salt. Let cool on pans for 10 minutes. Remove from pans, and let cool completely on wire racks. Store in an airtight container for up to 3 days.

CRANBERRY BARK

Makes 4 cups

10 ounces (300 grams) dark chocolate, finely chopped
½ teaspoon (1 gram) ground cinnamon
½ teaspoon (1 gram) ground allspice
¼ teaspoon ground cloves
1 cup (100 grams) fresh cranberries, room temperature, some chopped and some left whole
¼ cup (28 grams) chopped toasted hazelnuts
1 teaspoon (3 grams) flaked sea salt

1. Line a baking sheet with parchment paper.
2. In the top of a double boiler, combine chocolate, cinnamon, allspice, and cloves. Cook over simmering water, stirring frequently, until chocolate is melted.
3. Pour melted chocolate onto prepared pan. Using a spatula, spread to ⅛- to ¼-inch thickness. Immediately sprinkle with cranberries and hazelnuts, and gently press into chocolate. Sprinkle with flaked salt. Refrigerate or freeze until ready to use.

Photo by Rebecca Firth

GINGERBREAD CHAI COOKIES

Makes about 9 cookies

Packing a hit of chai and gingerbread spice, these aromatic wonders are rolled in a crystal coat of sparkling sugar for a touch of glitter and crunch.

½ cup (113 grams) unsalted butter, softened
¾ cup (150 grams) granulated sugar
1 teaspoon (4 grams) vanilla extract
1 large egg (50 grams)
¼ cup (85 grams) unsulphured molasses
2¼ cups (281 grams) all-purpose flour
1½ teaspoons (3 grams) Chai Spice (recipe follows)
1 teaspoon (5 grams) baking soda
1 teaspoon (2 grams) ground ginger
¼ teaspoon kosher salt
1 cup (200 grams) sparkling sugar

1. Preheat oven to 350°F (180°C). Line baking sheets with parchment paper.
2. In the bowl of a stand mixer fitted with the paddle attachment, beat butter, granulated sugar, and vanilla at medium speed until fluffy, 2 to 3 minutes, stopping to scrape sides of bowl. Beat in egg and molasses.
3. In a medium bowl, whisk together flour, Chai Spice, baking soda, ginger, and salt. With mixer on low speed, gradually add flour mixture to butter mixture, beating until well combined. Using a ¼-cup spring-loaded scoop, scoop dough, and shape into 2-inch balls. Roll balls in sparkling sugar, and place 2½ inches apart on prepared pans.
4. Bake until tops are cracked, 15 to 16 minutes. Let cool completely on wire racks.

CHAI SPICE
Makes about ½ cup

⅓ cup (32 grams) ground cardamom
2½ tablespoons (15 grams) ground cinnamon
4 teaspoons (8 grams) ground ginger
2 teaspoons (4 grams) ground cloves
2 teaspoons (4 grams) ground black pepper

1. In a small bowl, stir together all ingredients.

GINGER BOMBS

Makes 22 sandwich cookies

Recipe by Rebecca Firth

Come holiday season, I want everything all ginger, molasses, mistletoe, and sweet, and these Ginger Buttercream-stuffed molasses cookies encompass all of that (minus the greenery). They have heaps of ginger, but don't let the quantities scare you off—it's just the right amount.

1   cup (227 grams) unsalted butter, softened
1   cup (220 grams) firmly packed dark brown sugar
2   large eggs (100 grams), room temperature
1   large egg yolk (19 grams), room temperature
⅓   cup (113 grams) unsulphured molasses
1½   tablespoons (11 grams) grated fresh ginger
1   tablespoon (13 grams) vanilla extract
2   cups (264 grams) bread flour
1   cup (130 grams) all-purpose flour
1½   tablespoons (9 grams) ground ginger
2   teaspoons (10 grams) baking soda
2   teaspoons (4 grams) ground cinnamon
1   teaspoon (3 grams) sea salt
1   teaspoon (2 grams) ground cloves
Ginger Buttercream (recipe follows)

1. In the bowl of a stand mixer fitted with the paddle attachment, beat butter and brown sugar at medium speed until creamy, 2 to 3 minutes, stopping to scrape sides of bowl. Add eggs and egg yolk, one at a time, beating well after each addition. Add molasses, grated ginger, and vanilla, and beat for 1 minute.
2. In a medium bowl, whisk together flours, ground ginger, baking soda, cinnamon, sea salt, and cloves. With mixer on low speed, gradually add flour mixture to butter mixture, beating just until combined, about 1 minute. Using a spatula, scrape sides and bottom of bowl to ensure everything is incorporated. Shape dough into a disk, and wrap tightly in plastic wrap. Refrigerate until firm, about 1 hour.
3. Preheat oven to 350°F (180°C). Line several baking sheets with parchment paper.

4. Roll dough into 1-tablespoon (14-gram) balls, and place 2 inches apart on prepared pans. If dough is a little sticky, use 2 spoons or a cookie scoop to help.
5. Bake for 9 to 10 minutes. Let cool on pans for 5 minutes. Remove from pans, and let cool completely on wire racks. Spread Ginger Buttercream onto flat side of half of cookies. Place remaining cookies, flat side down, on top of filling. Store in an airtight container for up to 3 days.

GINGER BUTTERCREAM

Makes 2 cups

¼   cup (57 grams) unsalted butter, softened
2   ounces (55 grams) cream cheese, softened
2   cups (240 grams) confectioners' sugar
3   tablespoons (33 grams) finely minced candied ginger
1   tablespoon (15 grams) whole milk

1. In the bowl of a stand mixer fitted with the paddle attachment, beat butter, cream cheese, and confectioners' sugar at low speed until smooth and creamy, about 2 minutes. Add candied ginger and milk, and beat until milk is completely absorbed and small bits of candied ginger are visible throughout, about 1 minute. Use immediately.

Photo by Rebecca Firth

PALMIERS WITH VANILLA BEAN, PECAN, AND CARDAMOM

Makes about 36 cookies

Palmiers might just be the perfect cookie: crisp, buttery layers of puff pastry encased in caramelized sugar. It's hard to improve on something so classically perfect, but we think our version with cardamom, pecans, and vanilla bean seeds comes pretty close.

- ½   cup (100 grams) granulated sugar
- ½   cup (50 grams) pecan halves
- ½   teaspoon (1.5 grams) kosher salt
- ½   teaspoon (1 gram) ground cardamom
- ½   vanilla bean, split lengthwise, seeds scraped and reserved
- ½   (17.3-ounce) package (245 grams) frozen puff pastry, thawed

1. In the work bowl of a food processor, pulse together sugar, pecans, salt, cardamom, and vanilla bean seeds until mixture is uniformly incorporated and the texture of fine sand.

2. Pour half of sugar mixture onto a work surface. Place puff pastry on top, and sprinkle with additional sugar mixture. Begin rolling pastry, working quickly and incorporating more sugar mixture as needed (as you would when flouring your board while rolling piecrust or cookies). Roll up dough, jelly roll style, beginning with each long end and meeting in the middle. Freeze until firm, 10 to 15 minutes.

3. Line a baking sheet with parchment paper, and spritz with water.

4. Cut dough into ¼-inch-thick slices, and place about 2 inches apart on prepared pan. (See PRO TIP.) Freeze for 1 hour.

5. Preheat oven to 425°F (220°C).

6. Bake for 8 to 10 minutes, turning with a spatula halfway through baking. Let cool completely on a wire rack.

Photo by Stephen DeVries

PRO TIP
You will need to work in batches. It is OK to slice the entire log at once and place slices on a parchment paper-lined sheet pan in the freezer. Bake straight from the freezer about 12 at a time.

Makes 12 cookies

Think of these as our millenial pink version of retro Nabisco Mallomars.

Strawberry Marshmallow (recipe follows)
12 Strawberry Gingersnaps (recipe follows)
10 ounces (300 grams) dark chocolate melting wafers

1. Place a wire rack on a rimmed baking sheet.
2. Spoon Strawberry Marshmallow into a pastry bag fitted with a round piping tip (Wilton #2A). Using even pressure, pipe a "kiss" shape onto each Strawberry Gingersnap. Let stand until set, about 20 minutes.
3. In a medium microwave-safe bowl, microwave chocolate on high in 30-second intervals, stirring between each, until melted and smooth. Dip marshmallow-topped gingersnaps in melted chocolate, and place on prepared rack. (Melted chocolate can also be spooned over marshmallow if bowl is too shallow for dipping.) Let chocolate set. Store in an airtight container at room temperature for up to 5 days.

STRAWBERRY MARSHMALLOW

Makes 5 cups

⅔ cup (160 grams) water, divided
1   tablespoon plus ½ teaspoon (14 grams) unflavored gelatin
1¼ cups (250 grams) granulated sugar
⅔ cup (226 grams) light corn syrup
1½ cups (24 grams) freeze-dried strawberries

1. In the bowl of a stand mixer fitted with the whisk attachment, stir together ⅓ cup (80 grams) water and gelatin; let stand until softened, about 10 minutes.
2. In a large saucepan, combine granulated sugar, corn syrup, and remaining ⅓ cup (80 grams) water. Cook over medium-high heat until sugar is dissolved and a candy thermometer registers 240°F (116°C), about 6 minutes.
3. With mixer on low speed, slowly drizzle hot sugar mixture into gelatin mixture, beating just until combined. Increase mixer speed to medium, and beat until mixture begins to thicken, about 1 minute. Increase mixer speed to high, and beat until mixture turns very thick, white, and fluffy, about 10 minutes.
4. In the work bowl of a food processor, pulse freeze-dried strawberries until reduced to a powder. Add freeze-dried strawberries to marshmallow mixture, beating to combine.

STRAWBERRY GINGERSNAPS

Makes about 60 cookies

1   cup (227 grams) unsalted butter, softened
1⅓ cups (267 grams) granulated sugar
1   large egg (50 grams), room temperature
1   large egg yolk (19 grams), room temperature
½ teaspoon (2 grams) vanilla extract
⅓ cup (113 grams) molasses
3   cups (375 grams) all-purpose flour

CHOCOLATE-COVERED GINGER COOKIES
WITH STRAWBERRY MARSHMALLOW

½ cup (8 grams) freeze-dried strawberries, powdered
2½ teaspoons (12.5 grams) baking soda
2½ teaspoons (5 grams) ground cinnamon
2½ teaspoons (5 grams) ground ginger
¾ teaspoon (2.25 grams) kosher salt
¼ teaspoon ground black pepper
½ cup (48 grams) chopped Candied Strawberries (recipe follows)
¼ cup (43 grams) diced crystallized ginger

1. In the bowl of stand mixer fitted with the paddle attachment, beat butter and sugar at medium speed until fluffy, 3 to 4 minutes, stopping to scrape sides of bowl. Add egg, egg yolk, and vanilla, beating just until combined. Beat in molasses.
2. In a medium bowl, whisk together flour, powdered freeze-dried strawberries, baking soda, cinnamon, ground ginger, salt, and pepper. With mixer on low speed, gradually add flour mixture to butter mixture, beating just until combined. Add chopped Candied Strawberries and crystallized ginger, beating until combined.
3. On a heavily floured surface, divide dough in half. Shape each half into a 2-inch-wide log. Wrap tightly in plastic wrap, and freeze until firm, at least 1 hour.
4. Preheat oven to 325°F (170°C). Line 3 baking sheets with parchment paper.
5. Working with one log at a time, slice into ¼-inch-thick slices. Place on prepared pans.
6. Bake until edges are browned, 10 to 14 minutes. Let cool completely.

CANDIED STRAWBERRIES

Makes 1 cup

1   cup (200 grams) granulated sugar
½ cup (120 grams) water
½ cup (120 grams) fresh lemon juice
4   cups (680 grams) (⅛-inch-thick*) sliced fresh strawberries

1. In a small saucepan, bring sugar, ½ cup (120 grams) water, and lemon juice to a boil over medium heat; cook until sugar is dissolved. Remove from heat, and let cool completely.
2. Preheat oven to 200°F (93°C). Line 2 rimmed baking sheets with nonstick baking mats.
3. In a medium bowl, toss together sugar mixture and strawberries. Strain strawberries through a fine-mesh sieve. Place in a single layer on prepared pans. Gently pat strawberries with a paper towel to remove excess liquid.
4. Bake until dry but tacky, 2½ to 3 hours. Let cool completely. Cover and refrigerate for up to 1 week.

We used a mandoline to slice.

VANILLA CHAI PINWHEEL COOKIES

Makes 40 cookies

Recipe by Becky Sue Wilberding

Vanilla and chai-spiced cookie doughs are swirled together in a hypnotizing spiral of simple sweetness and aromatic spice with festive sparkling sugar edges.

2¾ cups (344 grams) all-purpose flour, divided
2 teaspoons (4 grams) ground cinnamon
1 teaspoon (2 grams) ground cardamom
¾ teaspoon (1.5 grams) ground ginger
1 teaspoon (5 grams) baking powder, divided
1 teaspoon (3 grams) kosher salt, divided
¼ teaspoon ground allspice
¼ teaspoon ground white pepper
½ cup (50 grams) pecan halves
1 cup (227 grams) unsalted butter, softened and divided
½ cup (110 grams) firmly packed light brown sugar
3 large eggs (150 grams), divided
2½ teaspoons (10 grams) vanilla extract, divided
½ cup (100 grams) granulated sugar
¼ cup (50 grams) sparkling or turbinado sugar

1. Preheat oven to 350°F (180°C).
2. In a medium bowl, whisk together 1¼ cups (156 grams) flour, cinnamon, cardamom, ginger, ½ teaspoon (2.5 grams) baking powder, ½ teaspoon (1.5 grams) salt, allspice, and white pepper. Set aside.
3. Arrange pecans on a baking sheet, and toast until they start to deepen in color, about 8 minutes. Let cool slightly. Transfer to the work bowl of a food processor. Add 2 tablespoons flour mixture, and pulse until pecans are finely ground. (The flour will absorb the oils from the nuts and will prevent a nut butter from forming in the food processor.) Add pecan mixture to remaining flour mixture, whisking to combine.
4. In the bowl of a stand mixer fitted with the paddle attachment, beat ½ cup (113.5 grams) butter and brown sugar at medium speed until creamy, 2 to 3 minutes, stopping to scrape sides of bowl. Add 1 egg (50 grams) and 1 teaspoon (4 grams) vanilla, beating until combined. With mixer on low speed, gradually add flour mixture,

beating until combined. Turn out dough onto a lightly floured surface, and shape into a disk. Wrap in plastic wrap, and refrigerate for at least 1 hour.
5. In the bowl of a stand mixer fitted with the paddle attachment, beat granulated sugar and remaining ½ cup (113.5 grams) butter at medium speed until creamy, 2 to 3 minutes, stopping to scrape sides of bowl. Add 1 egg (50 grams) and remaining 1½ teaspoons (6 grams) vanilla, beating until combined.
6. In a medium bowl, whisk together remaining 1½ cups (188 grams) flour, remaining ½ teaspoon (2.5 grams) baking powder, and remaining ½ teaspoon (1.5 grams) salt. With mixer on low speed, gradually add flour mixture to butter mixture, beating until combined. Turn out dough onto a lightly floured surface, and shape into a disk. Wrap in plastic wrap, and refrigerate for at least 1 hour.
7. Let doughs stand at room temperature until slightly softened, about 5 minutes. On a lightly floured sheet of parchment paper, roll vanilla cookie dough into a 16x12-inch rectangle, ⅛ inch thick. Transfer dough on parchment to a baking sheet. Refrigerate for 15 minutes. Repeat procedure with chai cookie dough.
8. Transfer vanilla cookie dough on parchment to a flat surface. Carefully invert chai cookie dough on top of vanilla cookie dough. Between sheets of parchment, gently roll over doughs a few times to press together. Peel away top sheet of parchment.
9. Starting at one long side, roll dough into a log, using parchment to help lift and roll. (If dough cracks, stop rolling, and let stand for a few minutes until pliable.) Be sure to roll doughs together as tightly as possible to avoid gaps. Tightly wrap in parchment paper, twisting ends to seal. Transfer to a baking sheet, seam side down. Refrigerate for at least 2 hours, or freeze until ready to use.
10. Preheat oven to 350°F (180°C). Line 2 baking sheets with parchment paper.
11. In a small bowl, whisk remaining 1 egg (50 grams). Brush log with egg wash, and sprinkle with sparkling or turbinado sugar. Roll back and forth a few times so sugar sticks to log. Using a sharp knife, cut into ¼-inch-thick slices. Place about 1 inch apart on prepared pans.
12. Bake on upper and middle racks of oven until edges are just beginning to turn golden, 12 to 15 minutes, rotating pans halfway through baking. Let cool completely on pans. Store in an airtight container for up to 2 weeks.

Note: *Dough can be refrigerated for up to 3 days or frozen for up to 1 month.*

Photo by Becky Sue Wilberding

PRO TIP
Use 1 to 2 paper towel rolls sliced lengthwise to keep the dough log from flattening on one side.

FIVE-SPICE GINGERBREAD COOKIES

Makes 35 to 65 cookies

Recipe by Rebecca Firth

Chinese five-spice powder is one of my favorite go-to spice blends. It has all of the usual flavors, like cinnamon and cloves, but also typically has Sichuan peppercorns for an added kick and fennel and star anise to keep things interesting. The five-spice is subtle in these, but feel free to add up to ½ teaspoon (1 gram) more to give these mega jazz hands.

¾   cup (170 grams) unsalted butter, softened
¾   cup (165 grams) firmly packed dark brown sugar
¾   cup (255 grams) unsulphured molasses
1   large egg (50 grams), room temperature
2   teaspoons (8 grams) vanilla extract
3⅔ cups (484 grams) bread flour
1   tablespoon (6 grams) ground ginger
2   teaspoons (4 grams) Chinese five-spice powder
1   teaspoon (3 grams) sea salt
½   teaspoon (1 gram) ground cinnamon
1½ cups (180 grams) confectioners' sugar
3 to 4 tablespoons (45 to 60 grams) whole milk
½   vanilla bean, split lengthwise, seeds scraped and reserved
Garnish: gold sprinkles

1. In the bowl of a stand mixer fitted with the paddle attachment, beat butter and brown sugar at medium speed until creamy, 2 to 3 minutes, stopping to scrape sides of bowl. With mixer on low speed, add molasses, and beat until well combined, about 1 minute. Add egg and vanilla, and beat for 1 minute.
2. In a medium bowl, whisk together flour, ginger, five-spice powder, salt, and cinnamon. Gradually add flour mixture to butter mixture, beating just until combined, about 1 minute. Using a spatula, scrape sides and bottom of bowl to ensure everything is incorporated. Shape dough into a disk, and wrap tightly in plastic wrap. Refrigerate for 15 minutes. (You want dough chilled but not so cold that it cracks when rolled out. If you refrigerate longer, let come closer to room temperature before rolling.)
3. Line a baking sheet with parchment paper.
4. On a lightly floured surface, roll dough to ¼- to ½-inch thickness. Add more flour as needed, and turn dough 90 degrees after each roll to keep sticking at bay. Place dough on prepared pan. Freeze for 10 minutes, or refrigerate for 20 minutes.
5. Position oven rack in top third of oven, no less than 6 inches from heat. Preheat oven to 350°F (180°C). Line several baking sheets with parchment paper.
6. Using a 1½-inch round cutter, cut dough, rerolling scraps as necessary. Place 1 inch apart on prepared pans. Freeze for 10 minutes, or refrigerate for 20 minutes.
7. Bake for 8 minutes. Let cool on pans for 5 minutes. Remove from pans, and let cool completely on wire racks.
8. In a small bowl, whisk together confectioners' sugar, milk, and vanilla bean seeds until smooth. Dip top of cooled cookies in glaze, letting excess drip off. Place cookies on wire rack, and immediately garnish with sprinkles, if desired. Let glaze set before serving. Store in an airtight container for up to 3 days.

Photo by Rebecca Firth

FIVE-SPICE PEANUT BUTTER COOKIES

Makes about 25 cookies

This recipe brings a little something new to the classic nutty cookie formula, blending the complementary notes of rich peanut butter and aromatic Chinese five-spice.

½ cup (113 grams) unsalted butter, softened
1 cup (220 grams) firmly packed dark brown sugar
1 large egg (50 grams)
½ cup (128 grams) crunchy peanut butter*
1 teaspoon (4 grams) vanilla extract
1½ cups (188 grams) all-purpose flour
¾ teaspoon (1.5 grams) Chinese five-spice powder
½ teaspoon (2.5 grams) baking powder
½ teaspoon (2.5 grams) baking soda
½ teaspoon (1 gram) ground cinnamon
¼ teaspoon kosher salt
½ cup (100 grams) granulated sugar

1. Line a baking sheet with parchment paper.
2. In the bowl of a stand mixer fitted with the paddle attachment, beat butter and brown sugar at medium speed until fluffy, 2 to 3 minutes, stopping to scrape sides of bowl. Add egg, beating well. Add peanut butter and vanilla, beating until combined.
3. In a medium bowl, whisk together flour, five-spice powder, baking powder, baking soda, cinnamon, and salt. With mixer on low speed, gradually add flour mixture to butter mixture, beating just until combined. Using a 1½-tablespoon spring-loaded scoop, scoop dough (about 28 grams each), and place on prepared pan. Refrigerate for 30 minutes.
4. Preheat oven to 350°F (180°C). Line 3 baking sheets with parchment paper.
5. Place granulated sugar in a small bowl. Roll each scoop of dough into a smooth ball, and toss in sugar, coating completely. Place 2½ inches apart on prepared pans. Press tines of a fork into surface of dough, creating a crosshatch design. Refrigerate for another 30 minutes.
6. Bake until light golden brown, 10 to 12 minutes, rotating pans halfway through baking. Let cool on pans for 5 minutes. Remove from pans, and let cool completely on wire racks.

We used JIF Natural Crunchy Peanut Butter.

CINNAMON ROLL PINWHEEL COOKIES

Makes about 28 cookies

Swirled with cinnamon sugar and drizzled with a sweet glaze, this crumbly cookie-cinnamon roll hybrid brings you the best of both worlds.

⅔ cup (150 grams) unsalted butter, softened
⅔ cup (133 grams) plus 2 tablespoons (24 grams) granulated sugar, divided
1 large egg (50 grams)
2 teaspoons (8 grams) vanilla extract
1¾ cups (219 grams) all-purpose flour
1 tablespoon (6 grams) plus 1 teaspoon (2 grams) ground cinnamon, divided
½ teaspoon (1.5 grams) kosher salt
¼ teaspoon (1.25 grams) baking powder
¼ teaspoon (1.25 grams) baking soda
2 tablespoons (28 grams) firmly packed light brown sugar
2 tablespoons (28 grams) unsalted butter, melted
Sugar Glaze (recipe follows)

1. In the bowl of a stand mixer fitted with the paddle attachment, beat softened butter and ⅔ cup (133 grams) granulated sugar at medium speed until creamy, 2 to 3 minutes, stopping to scrape sides of bowl. Add egg, beating well. Beat in vanilla.
2. In a medium bowl, whisk together flour, 1 teaspoon (2 grams) cinnamon, salt, baking powder, and baking soda. With mixer on low speed, gradually add flour mixture to butter mixture, beating until combined. Shape dough into a disk, and wrap in plastic wrap. Refrigerate for 1 hour.
3. Between 2 sheets of parchment paper, roll dough into a 14x9-inch rectangle, about ¼ inch thick. Transfer dough between parchment to refrigerator. Refrigerate for 30 minutes.
4. In a small bowl, stir together brown sugar, remaining 2 tablespoons (24 grams) granulated sugar, and remaining 1 tablespoon (6 grams) cinnamon. Remove top sheet of parchment from dough, and brush with melted butter. Sprinkle with cinnamon sugar mixture. Starting at one long side, tightly roll up dough, jelly roll style, using parchment to help lift and roll. Wrap log in parchment, and freeze for at least 1 hour.

5. Line 2 baking sheets with parchment paper.
6. Cut dough into ½-inch-thick slices. Place 1 inch apart on prepared pans. Freeze for at least 30 minutes.
7. Preheat oven to 350°F (180°C).
8. Bake until bottom edges start to brown, 8 to 10 minutes. Let cool on pans for 1 minute. Remove from pans, and let cool completely on wire racks. Drizzle with Sugar Glaze. Let set before serving.

SUGAR GLAZE
Makes about ½ cup

1 cup (120 grams) confectioners' sugar
2 tablespoons (30 grams) whole milk

1. In a small bowl, whisk together confectioners' sugar and milk until smooth. Use immediately.

STAMPED SPECULAAS COOKIES

Makes about 17 cookies

Our homemade stamped version of everyone's favorite airplane treat will remind you why this is the reigning emperor of spice cookies.

1	cup (227 grams) unsalted butter, softened
½	cup (110 grams) firmly packed dark brown sugar
1	tablespoon (21 grams) molasses
1	teaspoon (4 grams) vanilla extract
1¾	cups (219 grams) all-purpose flour
1	cup (135 grams) graham flour
1½	teaspoons (3 grams) ground cinnamon
¾	teaspoon (3.75 grams) baking soda
½	teaspoon (1.5 grams) kosher salt
½	cup (100 grams) granulated sugar

1. Line a baking sheet with parchment paper.

2. In the bowl of a stand mixer fitted with the paddle attachment, beat butter and brown sugar at medium speed until creamy, 2 to 3 minutes, stopping to scrape sides of bowl. Beat in molasses and vanilla.

3. In a medium bowl, whisk together flours, cinnamon, baking soda, and salt. With mixer on low speed, gradually add flour mixture to butter mixture, beating until combined. Using a 1.5-ounce spring-loaded scoop, scoop dough, and place on prepared pan. Cover and refrigerate for 1 hour.

4. Preheat oven to 350°F (180°C). Line 3 baking sheets with parchment paper.

5. With floured hands, roll each scoop of dough into a ball (about 40 grams each). Roll balls in granulated sugar, coating completely. Press into a flat disk about 1½ inches wide. Place about 3 inches apart on prepared pans. Using a floured cookie stamp*, press down on dough until dough just barely meets edges of stamp.

6. Bake until bottom edges start to brown, about 12 minutes. Let cool on pans for 5 minutes. Remove from pans, and let cool completely on wire racks.

*We used Nordic Ware Geo Cast Cookie Stamps and All Season Cast Cookie Stamps, available at nordicware.com.

BAKE IT
BIGGER

FROM A 9-INCH BIRTHDAY PARTY-READY
COOKIE PACKED WITH RAINBOW SPRINKLES TO
A DOUBLE-CHOCOLATE SKILLET SENSATION,
THESE RECIPES PROVE THAT WHEN IT COMES
TO COOKIES, THE BIGGER, THE BETTER

THE ULTIMATE SUGAR COOKIES

Makes about 22 cookies

Soft, simple, and epically large, this has all the comfort you could want from a sparkling sugar cookie, only twice as big.

1	cup (227 grams) unsalted butter, softened
1¼	cups (250 grams) granulated sugar
½	cup (60 grams) confectioners' sugar
2	large eggs (100 grams)
¼	cup (60 grams) sour cream
2	teaspoons (8 grams) vanilla extract
1½	cups (188 grams) all-purpose flour
1	cup (125 grams) cake flour
½	teaspoon (2.5 grams) baking powder
½	teaspoon (2.5 grams) baking soda
½	teaspoon (1.5 grams) kosher salt
3	tablespoons (36 grams) sparkling white sugar

1. Preheat oven to 350°F (180°C). Line 4 baking sheets with parchment paper.
2. In the bowl of a stand mixer fitted with the paddle attachment, beat butter, granulated sugar, and confectioners' sugar at medium speed until fluffy, 2 to 3 minutes, stopping to scrape sides of bowl. Add eggs, one at a time, beating well after each addition. Beat in sour cream and vanilla.
3. In a medium bowl, whisk together flours, baking powder, baking soda, and salt. With mixer on low speed, gradually add flour mixture to butter mixture, beating just until combined. Using a 3-tablespoon spring-loaded scoop, scoop dough (about 44 grams each), and place 4 inches apart on prepared pans. Top with sparkling sugar.
4. Bake until edges are lightly browned, 12 to 14 minutes. Let cool on pans for 5 minutes. Remove from pans, and let cool completely on wire racks.

TAHINI-CARDAMOM SHORTBREAD WITH PISTACHIOS

Makes 30 cookies

Recipe by Ben Mims

Tahini is a natural match with shortbread because its slight drying effect produces a crumbly texture in baked goods, a boon to shortbread. This version adds buttery pistachios for color and crunch. A thick coating of confectioners' sugar sprinkled as soon as the cookies come out of the oven melds to the top, creating a snow-white, sweet layer to the nutty-toasty cookies.

⅔	cup (133 grams) granulated sugar
½	teaspoon (1.5 grams) kosher salt
¼	teaspoon ground cardamom
1	cup (227 grams) unsalted butter, softened
¼	cup (56 grams) tahini
3	cups (375 grams) all-purpose flour
⅓	cup (38 grams) roughly chopped pistachios
½	cup (60 grams) confectioners' sugar

1. Preheat oven to 325°F (170°C). Line a 13x9-inch baking pan with parchment paper, letting excess extend over sides of pan.
2. In the bowl of a stand mixer fitted with the paddle attachment, stir together granulated sugar, salt, and cardamom. With mixer on medium speed, add butter and tahini, beating until smooth, about 1 minute. Add flour, beating just until combined and crumbly. Reduce mixer speed to low, and beat for 10 minutes. (This amount of time helps develop some gluten, which you want to create the characteristic brittle texture of the shortbread.) Beat in pistachios.

3. Transfer dough to prepared pan, pressing into bottom. Using a paring knife, score dough into 2¼x1½-inch rectangles. Prick dough all over with a fork, being careful to stay within lines of rectangles.
4. Bake until very light golden brown at the edges, about 40 minutes. Transfer pan to a wire rack, and cut along scored lines to separate rectangles while dough is still hot. Immediately dust top with confectioners' sugar. Let cool completely in pan. Using excess parchment as handles, gently remove from pan, and break apart to serve.

Photo and styling by Mason + Dixon

OUR BEST SKILLET COOKIE

Makes 1 (10-inch) cookie

With melted chocolate, old-fashioned oats, and rich peanut butter, this is the ultimate indulgent treat.

1   cup (227 grams) unsalted butter, softened
1½   cups (330 grams) firmly packed light brown sugar
1   large egg (50 grams), room temperature
2   teaspoons (8 grams) vanilla extract
1½   cups (188 grams) all-purpose flour
1½   teaspoons (7.5 grams) baking powder
½   teaspoon (1.5 grams) kosher salt
1¼   cups (100 grams) old-fashioned oats, divided
2   tablespoons (30 grams) whole milk
¾   cup (192 grams) creamy peanut butter
⅔   cup (113 grams) semisweet chocolate chips

1. Preheat oven to 325°F (170°C). Butter and flour a 10-inch cast-iron skillet.
2. In the bowl of a stand mixer fitted with the paddle attachment, beat butter and brown sugar at medium speed until fluffy, 3 to 4 minutes, stopping to scrape sides of bowl. Add egg and vanilla; beat until combined.
3. In a medium bowl, whisk together flour, baking powder, and salt. With mixer on low speed, gradually add flour mixture to butter mixture, beating just until combined. Beat in ¾ cup (60 grams) oats and milk.
4. With dampened hands, press half of dough into bottom of prepared skillet. Spread peanut butter onto dough. Drop heaping tablespoonfuls of remaining dough over peanut butter. Sprinkle with chocolate chips and remaining ½ cup (40 grams) oats.
5. Bake until golden brown, about 45 minutes, loosely covering with foil during last 10 minutes of baking to prevent excess browning, if necessary. Let cool for 15 minutes before serving.

SPRINKLE SUGAR COOKIE

Makes 1 (9-inch) cookie

When it comes to celebrations, it's go big or go home. Packed with rainbow sprinkles and baked in a 9-inch springform pan, this giant cookie is birthday party-ready.

¾ cup (170 grams) unsalted butter, softened
½ cup (110 grams) firmly packed light brown sugar
½ cup (100 grams) granulated sugar
1 large egg (50 grams)
1 tablespoon (13 grams) vanilla extract
1 cup (127 grams) bread flour
1 cup (125 grams) all-purpose flour
2 teaspoons (10 grams) baking powder
½ teaspoon (1.5 grams) kosher salt
¼ teaspoon (1.25 grams) baking soda
¼ teaspoon ground nutmeg
⅓ cup (59 grams) plus 1 tablespoon (10 grams) rainbow sprinkles*, divided
Buttercream (recipe follows)
Garnish: sprinkles

1. Preheat oven to 350°F (180°C). Butter and flour a 9-inch springform pan; line bottom of pan with parchment paper.
2. In the bowl of a stand mixer fitted with the paddle attachment, beat butter and sugars at medium speed until fluffy, 2 to 3 minutes, stopping to scrape sides of bowl. Add egg, beating well. Beat in vanilla.
3. In a medium bowl, whisk together flours, baking powder, salt, baking soda, and nutmeg. With mixer on low speed, gradually add flour mixture to butter mixture, beating until combined. Using a rubber spatula, gently fold in ⅓ cup (59 grams) sprinkles. Spread batter into prepared pan, smoothing top with an offset spatula. Sprinkle with remaining 1 tablespoon (10 grams) sprinkles.
4. Bake until center is set and a wooden pick inserted in center comes out clean, 25 to 27 minutes. Let cool in pan for 10 minutes. Remove sides of pan, and let cool completely on base.
5. Place half of Buttercream in a pastry bag fitted with a French star #4B tip. Place remaining Buttercream in a pastry bag fitted with a round #12 tip. Alternate piping stars and rounds around edge of cookie. Top with sprinkles, if desired.

We used Betty Crocker Rainbow Sprinkles.

BUTTERCREAM

Makes about 1 cup

¼ cup (57 grams) unsalted butter, softened
1½ cups (180 grams) confectioners' sugar
1 tablespoon plus 2 teaspoons (25 grams) heavy whipping cream
½ teaspoon (3 grams) vanilla bean paste
¼ teaspoon kosher salt

1. In the bowl of a stand mixer fitted with the paddle attachment, beat butter at medium speed until smooth. Gradually add confectioners' sugar, beating until smooth. With mixer on low speed, add cream, vanilla bean paste, and salt, beating until combined. Increase mixer speed to medium, and beat for 30 seconds. Use immediately.

PRO TIP
Gently folding in the sprinkles is important to minimize breakage and bleeding during baking.

CHOCOLATE GINGER SUGAR COOKIES

Makes 12 cookies

Recipe by Sarah Kieffer

Sugar cookies are great on their own, but add cocoa powder, crystallized ginger, dark chocolate, and more butter, and they become an incredible and unique addition to any holiday table.

1	cup (227 grams) unsalted butter, softened
2¼	cups (450 grams) granulated sugar, divided
1	large egg (50 grams)
1	teaspoon (4 grams) vanilla extract
2	cups (250 grams) all-purpose flour
½	cup (43 grams) natural cocoa powder or a combination cocoa powder*
1	teaspoon (2 grams) ground ginger
¾	teaspoon (3.75 grams) baking soda
½	teaspoon (1.5 grams) kosher salt
4	ounces (115 grams) semisweet chocolate, chopped
¼	cup (41 grams) chopped crystallized ginger

1. Preheat oven to 350°F (180°C). Line 2 baking sheets with parchment paper.

2. In the bowl of a stand mixer fitted with the paddle attachment, beat butter at medium speed until smooth. Add 1¾ cups (350 grams) sugar, and beat until fluffy, 2 to 3 minutes. Add egg and vanilla, and beat until combined.

3. In a medium bowl, combine flour, cocoa, ground ginger, baking soda, and salt. With mixer on low speed, gradually add flour mixture to butter mixture, beating just until combined. Stir in chopped chocolate and crystallized ginger.

4. Place remaining ½ cup (100 grams) sugar in a medium bowl. Shape dough into 12 (85-gram) balls (a scant ⅓ cup each). Roll each ball in sugar, and place 6 cookies, 2 inches apart, on each prepared pan.

5. Bake, one batch at a time, until edges are set and centers are puffed and starting to crackle, 11 to 14 minutes. Let cool completely on pans. Refrigerate in an airtight container for up to 3 days.

*We used Hershey's Special Dark Cocoa.

Photo by Sarah Kieffer

CHOCOLATE CHIP SKILLET COOKIE

Makes 1 (10-inch) cookie

Get creative with this infinitely customizable skillet cookie. We used walnuts, bittersweet chocolate, and milk chocolate, but any mix-ins you have in your pantry will work. Dried fruit, oats, the last of your holiday candy, or leftover coffee grounds are fair game. You can even swirl in your favorite spreads, like peanut butter or Nutella.

¾ cup (170 grams) unsalted butter, softened
¾ cup (165 grams) firmly packed light brown sugar
¾ cup (255 grams) maple syrup
2 teaspoons (8 grams) vanilla extract
1 large egg (50 grams)
1 large egg yolk (19 grams)
2¼ cups (281 grams) all-purpose flour
½ teaspoon (2.5 grams) baking soda
½ teaspoon (1.5 grams) kosher salt
¾ cup (85 grams) chopped walnuts, divided
⅔ cup (113 grams) chopped bittersweet chocolate, divided
⅔ cup (113 grams) chopped milk chocolate, divided

1. Preheat oven to 350°F (180°C). Butter and flour a 10-inch cast-iron skillet.
2. In the bowl of a stand mixer fitted with the paddle attachment, beat butter and brown sugar at medium speed until creamy, 3 to 4 minutes, stopping to scrape sides of bowl. Add maple syrup and vanilla, and beat until well combined, about 1 minute. Add egg and egg yolk, and beat until well combined.
3. In a medium bowl, whisk together flour, baking soda, and salt. With mixer on low speed, gradually add flour mixture to butter mixture, beating until combined. Beat in ½ cup (57 grams) walnuts, ½ cup (85 grams) bittersweet chocolate, and ½ cup (85 grams) milk chocolate. Spoon batter into prepared skillet.
4. Bake until golden brown and center is just set, 40 to 50 minutes, loosely covering with foil halfway through baking. (Begin checking cookie closely for doneness starting at 40 minutes.) Sprinkle with remaining ¼ cup (28 grams) walnuts, remaining bittersweet chocolate, and remaining milk chocolate. Cover with foil, and bake 5 minutes more. Let cool on a wire rack. Serve warm or at room temperature.

Note: *If substituting mix-ins, use the same measurement of any nut or chocolate you have available.*

OATMEAL CREAM SANDWICH COOKIES

Makes about 12 sandwich cookies

Little Debbie Oatmeal Creme Pies were hands down my childhood favorite. To this day, they're my official road trip food that I always stop for at a gas station. Bigger and better than store-bought but just as nostalgia-inducing, these jumbo oatmeal cream pie cookies prove you can never have too much of a good thing.

3   cups (274 grams) quick-cooking oats
1½   cups (188 grams) all-purpose flour
2   tablespoons (10 grams) unsweetened cocoa powder
1¾   teaspoons (4.5 grams) kosher salt, divided
1   teaspoon (2 grams) ground cinnamon
½   teaspoon (2.5 grams) baking soda
2   cups (454 grams) unsalted butter, softened and divided
1½   cups (330 grams) firmly packed dark brown sugar
⅓   cup (67 grams) granulated sugar
2   large eggs (100 grams)
1   tablespoon (21 grams) molasses
1   tablespoon (21 grams) dark corn syrup
1   teaspoon (4 grams) vanilla extract
½   cup (64 grams) finely chopped raisins
1   teaspoon (6 grams) vanilla bean paste
4   cups (480 grams) confectioners' sugar
1   tablespoon (15 grams) whole milk

1. In the work bowl of a food processor, pulse oats until almost ground but not powdery. Add flour, cocoa, 1½ teaspoons (4.5 grams) salt, cinnamon, and baking soda; pulse just until combined. Set aside.

2. In the bowl of a stand mixer fitted with the paddle attachment, beat 1 cup (227 grams) butter, brown sugar, and granulated sugar at medium speed until fluffy, 2 to 3 minutes, stopping to scrape sides of bowl. Add eggs, one at a time, beating well after each addition. Beat in molasses, corn syrup, and vanilla extract until combined. With mixer on low speed, gradually add oats mixture, beating until combined. Stir in raisins. Cover and refrigerate for 30 minutes.

3. Preheat oven to 350°F (180°C). Line several baking sheets with parchment paper.

4. Shape dough into 24 (1½-inch) balls (about 54 grams each), and place 3 inches apart on prepared pans.

5. Bake until cookies flatten and turn deep golden brown, 10 to 11 minutes. (Do not overbake.) Let cool on pans for 5 minutes. Remove from pans, and let cool completely on wire racks.

6. In the bowl of a stand mixer fitted with the paddle attachment, beat vanilla bean paste, remaining 1 cup (227 grams) butter, and remaining ¼ teaspoon salt at medium speed until well combined. Reduce mixer speed to low. Gradually add confectioners' sugar, beating until smooth. Beat in milk until smooth. Pipe or spread about ¼ cup (60 grams) filling onto flat side of half of cookies. Place remaining cookies, flat side down, on top of filling.

PRO TIP
To pipe the filling with the traditional scalloped edges, transfer filling to a large pastry bag fitted with a large round tip (#1A). Pipe teardrop-shaped dollops onto flat side of half of cookies, beginning each dollop at the edge of the cookie and ending near the center.

CHOCOLATE PECAN SKILLET COOKIE

Makes 1 (10-inch) cookie

Chocolate decadence at its finest, this skillet cookie is filled and topped with molten bittersweet chocolate and warm, toasted pecans. Dive in with a spoon—you won't want to waste time cutting this into wedges.

¾ cup (170 grams) unsalted butter, softened
1½ cups (300 grams) granulated sugar
2 large eggs (100 grams)
2 teaspoons (8 grams) vanilla extract
1½ cups (188 grams) all-purpose flour
¼ cup (21 grams) unsweetened cocoa powder
½ teaspoon (2.5 grams) baking soda
½ teaspoon (1.5 grams) kosher salt
8 ounces (225 grams) 60% cacao bittersweet chocolate, roughly chopped
⅓ cup (38 grams) plus 2 tablespoons (14 grams) chopped toasted pecans, divided

1. Preheat oven to 350°F (180°C). Butter and flour a 10-inch cast-iron skillet.
2. In the bowl of a stand mixer fitted with the paddle attachment, beat butter and sugar at medium speed until fluffy, 2 to 3 minutes, stopping to scrape sides of bowl. Add eggs, one at a time, beating well after each addition. Beat in vanilla.
3. In a medium bowl, whisk together flour, cocoa, baking soda, and salt. With mixer on low speed, gradually add flour mixture to butter mixture, beating until combined. Stir in 4 ounces (112.5 grams) of chocolate and ⅓ cup (38 grams) pecans. Spread batter into prepared pan.
4. Bake until puffed and a wooden pick inserted in center comes out with very moist crumbs, about 35 minutes. (Do not overbake.) Top warm cookie with remaining 4 ounces (112.5 grams) chocolate and remaining 2 tablespoons (14 grams) pecans. Bake 2 minutes more. Let cool for 1 hour before serving.

recipe index

credits

Editorial
Editor-in-Chief Brian Hart Hoffman
VP/Culinary & Custom Content
Brooke Michael Bell
Group Creative Director Deanna Rippy Gardner
Managing Editor Sophia Jones
Associate Editor Kyle Grace Mills
Assistant Editor Lillie Mermoud
Copy Editor Meg Lundberg
Recipe Editor Fran Jensen

Food Stylists/Recipe Developers
Laura Crandall, Ashley Jones, Elizabeth Stringer

Stylists
Sidney Bragiel, Mary Beth Jones, Beth K. Seeley

Photographers
Jim Bathie, William Dickey, Nicole Du Bois,
Mac Jamieson, Stephanie Welbourne Steele

Contributing Photographers
Kassie Borreson, Matt Armendariz,
Mason + Dixon

Contributing Recipe Developers/Food Stylists
Marian Cooper Cairns, Kellie Kelly, Ben Mims,
Jenn Yee

**Contributing Recipe Developers/Food Stylists/
Photographers**
Erin Clarkson, Rebecca Firth, Zoë François,
Laura Kasavan, Sarah Kieffer, Edd Kimber,
Joshua Weissman, Becky Sue Wilberding

Cover
Photography by William Dickey
Recipe Development & Food Styling
by Laura Crandall
Styling by Caroline Blum

Pages 2-3 Photography by Matt Armendariz
Pages 4-5 Photography by Matt Armendariz
Pages 6, 7 Photography by Edd Kimber
Page 30 Photography by Sarah Kieffer
Page 63 Photography by Laura Kasavan
Page 83 Photography by Joshua Weissman
Page 152 Photography by Rebecca Firth